Your Baby's First Year

By the Editors of Time-Life Books

Alexandria, Virginia

TIME
LIFE
BOOKS

Time-Life Books Inc.
is a wholly owned subsidiary of

Time Incorporated

FOUNDER: Henry R. Luce 1898-1967

Editor-in-Chief: Henry Anatole Grunwald
Chairman and Chief Executive Officer:
J. Richard Munro
President and Chief Operating Officer:
N. J. Nicholas Jr.
Chairman of the Executive Committee:
Ralph P. Davidson
Corporate Editor: Ray Cave
Group Vice President, Books: Reginald K. Brack Jr.
Vice President, Books: George Artandi

Time-Life Books Inc.

EDITOR: George Constable
Director of Design: Louis Klein
Director of Editorial Resources: Phyllis K. Wise
Acting Text Director: Ellen Phillips
Editorial Board: Russell B. Adams Jr., Dale M.
Brown, Roberta Conlan, Thomas H. Flaherty, Donia
Ann Steele, Rosalind Stubenberg, Kit van Tulleken,
Henry Woodhead
Director of Photography and Research:
John Conrad Weiser

PRESIDENT: Reginald K. Brack Jr.
Executive Vice Presidents: John M. Fahey Jr.,
Christopher T. Linen
Senior Vice Presidents: James L. Mercer,
Leopoldo Toralballa
Vice Presidents: Stephen L. Bair, Ralph J. Cuomo,
Terence J. Furlong, Neal Goff, Stephen L. Goldstein,
Juanita T. James, Hallett Johnson III, Robert H.
Smith, Paul R. Stewart
Director of Production Services:
Robert J. Passantino

Library of Congress Cataloguing-in-Publication Data
Your baby's first year.
   (Successful parenting)
   Bibliography: p.
   Includes index.
   1. Infants — Care and hygiene. 2. Parenting.
3. Child rearing. 4. Child development.
I. Time-Life Books. II. Series.
HQ774.Y69 1986   649'.122   86-22983
ISBN 0-8094-5904-3
ISBN 0-8094-5905-1 (lib. bdg.)

Successful Parenting

SERIES DIRECTOR: Donia Ann Steele
Deputy Editor: Jim Hicks
Series Administrator: Norma E. Shaw
Editorial Staff for *Your Baby's First Year:*
Designer: Raymond Ripper
Picture Editor: Neil Kagan
Text Editor: Robert A. Doyle
Staff Writer: Janet Cave
Researchers: Fran Moshos, Nancy C. Scott
(principals), Patricia N. McKinney
Copy Coordinators: Marfé Ferguson,
Carolee Belkin Walker
Picture Coordinator: Bradley Hower
Editorial Assistant: Jenester C. Lewis

Special Contributors: Amy Goodwin Aldrich,
Charlotte Anker, Lynne Bair, Pat Daniels, George
Daniels, Ray Jones, John Manners, Brian Miller,
Carolyn Mooney, James G. Moore, Brian McGinn,
Wendy Murphy, Susan Perry, Jane Anne Peterson,
Gerry Schremp (text); Anne Munoz Furlong, Melva
Holloman, Rita Mullin, Beth Py, Ann Ready
(research); John Drummond, Jennifer Gilman,
Kenneth E. Hancock, Susan K. White (design).

Editorial Operations
Copy Chief: Diane Ullius
Editorial Operations: Caroline A. Boubin
(manager)
Production: Celia Beattie
Library: Louise D. Forstall

Correspondents: Elisabeth Kraemer-Singh (Bonn);
Maria Vincenza Aloisi (Paris); Ann Natanson
(Rome).

First printing. Printed in U.S.A.

Published simultaneously in Canada.
School and library distribution by
Silver Burdett Company, Morristown,
New Jersey 07960.

TIME-LIFE is a trademark of Time
Incorporated U.S.A.

Other Publications

*For information on and a full description
of any of the Time-Life Books series listed
above, please write:*
Reader Information
Time-Life Books
541 North Fairbanks Court
Chicago, Illinois 60611

This volume is one of a series about raising children.

The Consultants

General Consultant

Dr. Lewis P. Lipsitt, overall consultant for *Your Baby's First Year,* is a professor of psychology and of medical science at Brown University, and he is Director of the university's Child Study Center. Dr. Lipsitt has been a Guggenheim Fellow, a fellow at the Center for Advanced Study in the Behavioral Sciences at Stanford University and a visiting scientist at the National Institute of Mental Health. He has served on many national advisory boards, and he has lectured and written extensively on all aspects of infant behavior and development.

Special Consultants

Dr. Gordon B. Avery, a pediatrician and neonatologist, contributed to the section on the newborn. Dr. Avery is a professor of child health and development and Director of the Division of Neonatology at George Washington University School of Medicine. He is also Chairman of the Department of Neonatology at Children's Hospital National Medical Center in Washington, D.C. He has done extensive research and writing in newborn health and development, and he is editor of the textbook *Neonatology: Pathophysiology and Management of the Newborn.*

Dr. Constance H. Keefer, who consulted on the subjects of health, safety and everyday baby care, is a pediatrician with the Harvard Community Health Plan and an instructor in pediatrics and primary care at Harvard Medical School. In addition to her teaching work, Dr. Keefer is currently researching cross-cultural child-rearing practices in collaboration with anthropologists for the Harvard School of Public Health and the HCHP. Dr. Keefer is the former supervisor of the Early Childhood Program Clinic at Children's Hospital Medical Center in Boston. She has also been a featured speaker at the National Center for Clinical Infant Programs in Washington, D.C.

Dr. Marshall H. Klaus, an expert on infant health care and the subject of parent-infant bonding, contributed to the section on newborns. Dr. Klaus is Professor and Chairman of the Department of Pediatrics and Human Development at Michigan State University. He has done considerable research on the care of infants and their families, and he is the co-author of *Care of the High-Risk Infant, Parent-Infant Bonding* and *The Amazing Newborn.*

Dr. Buford L. Nichols Jr., Professor of Pediatrics and Physiology at Baylor College of Medicine in Houston, consulted on nutritional issues for the book. Dr. Nichols is also Director of the USDA Children's Nutrition Research Center in Houston, and he has written numerous articles on the role of nutrition in child health.

Dr. Joseph Sparling, an expert on the subject of toys and curriculum materials for young children, assisted with the activities in the developmental section of this book. He is an educational psychologist currently serving as a senior research investigator at the Frank Porter Graham Child Development Center of the University of North Carolina at Chapel Hill, and he is a lecturer in the School of Education at the university. Dr. Sparling's published work includes *Learningames for the First Three Years* and *Partners for Learning.*

Dr. Marc Weissbluth, who contributed the material on colic, is an associate professor of pediatrics at Northwestern University Medical School and Director of the Sleep Disorders Center at Children's Memorial Hospital in Chicago. Dr. Weissbluth has lectured and written widely on the subjects of colic, crying and infant sleep patterns, and he is the author of *Crybabies: Coping with Colic.*

Contents

4   Health and Safety   84

5   A Year of Remarkable Development   98

From Pregnancy to Parenthood

New parents today are, undoubtedly, better prepared for childbirth than any generation of parents before. Books and magazines offer insights into the psychological dimensions of parenthood, while in prenatal classes, mothers-to-be go through detailed rehearsals of labor and delivery, and prospective fathers get hands-on practice in changing diapers and other baby-care tasks. Tests administered during pregnancy allow doctors to monitor the health of the unborn child and can even give parents advance news of the baby's sex.

The truth is, however, that having a baby is an experience that a prospective parent can never be totally prepared for. Until the actual moment arrives, there is no way of knowing how your body will withstand night after night of interrupted sleep. No book or class can fully prepare a mother for the great adventure of breast-feeding or predict a father's emotions as he holds his son or daughter for the first time.

One of the most surprising revelations about life with a newborn is discovering the way in which time seems to slip out of joint. Day and night tend to blend together, marked off not by the sun rising and setting, but by the sporadic, round-the-clock cycle of the baby's eating, sleeping and fussing periods. For some first-time parents temporarily set back by the anxieties of adjustment and feelings of physical and emotional fatigue, days at home with a newborn seem to drag out interminably, and the dominant feeling is one of simply hanging on.

Time does pass, nevertheless, and with it your baby grows swiftly out of the unsettled, newborn phase and into patterns that are fairly predictable and quite manageable. If you are typical, in a few months' time you will be looking back on those early days with amusement and even a little nostalgia, marveling at how quickly they actually flew by. So, if you are wise, you will cherish the newborn days while you can — as a special time in your child's life that will never come again.

The Experience of Birth

From the moment your baby begins his journey toward the light, the experience of birth can truly be described as sensational. Leaving the warm, fluid-filled and essentially weightless haven of the womb, he enters the tight, muscular birth canal, where he is pushed, inch by inch, toward the cervical opening.

Meeting the world head-first
The baby's head, fitting snugly in its passage through the mother's pelvic opening, usually takes the lead. As the contractions come, the skull's unfused bones squeeze together and overlap slightly, the ears fold and the nose flattens. With the front of his body facing the mother's backbone for maximum flexibility, a baby's arms and legs stretch and bend in many ways to aid his passage. The once-steady flow of oxygen decreases slightly as the umbilical cord connecting him to his mother's supply system is compressed.

At the climactic moment of birth, when all the forces propelling him outward reach their peak, the infant first feels the touch of human hands in the doctor's firm grasp. For the first time, too, he experiences cold and sees bright light.

The infant's lifeline to all that was familiar is cut, both literally and figuratively, as the umbilical cord is severed. It is no wonder that so many babies enter the world crying!

Despite his protests and fragile appearance, this new creature is a complete person, amazingly strong and remarkably competent. Much of what he needs to do now he has been practicing in the uterus, and the mechanisms for those functions that he has not yet had to perform are ready to start.

The first breaths
In the womb, a baby's modest oxygen needs were provided by his mother through the nourishing conduit of the placenta and umbilical cord. Seconds after the separation of birth, the newborn's lungs must inflate and draw air for the first time. Usually, the many changes that accompany birth are enough to trigger the respiratory reflex and prompt the baby's first deep breath. If not, the obstetrician may tap the infant's heels together or gently rub his body to move the chest muscles into action and inflate the lungs.

The physical effort required to draw air for the first time through respiratory passages that are filled with secretions and amniotic fluid can be enormous, but most babies manage on their own. If your baby is still struggling for adequate air after two or three gasps, your doctor will probably suction the mouth and nose with a bulb syringe to aid in clearing the airway.

At the same time, the newborn undergoes profound and rapid changes in his circulatory system. With the detachment of the placenta from the mother and the severing of the umbilical cord, a baby's own system is forced to take over the oxygenation and cleansing of blood. The newborn abandons the simple blood circuit of the fetal state for the far more sophisticated circulatory system that lay in readiness — one that will now send nearly all the blood to the lungs to pick up oxygen

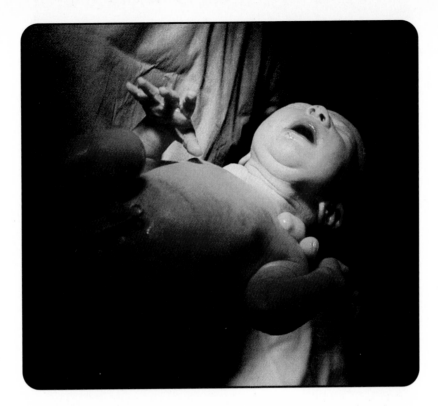

before pumping it around the body. Accustomed in the mother's womb to a placental blood flow of only one pint per minute, the newborn is soon pumping almost double that amount around his entire vascular system on his own.

The digestive tract's debut

Responsibility for digestion and the clearing of wastes also shifts from mother to baby at the instant of birth. Up to now the baby has never known a moment's hunger; nourishment has been sent her way automatically. Now she must breathe, take in milk and swallow it — all in the right sequence.

Fortunately, the infant arrives with a strong sucking reflex as well as the mechanisms necessary for swallowing and digesting milk. The newborn's sphincter muscles also are programmed to respond to pressure so that when her bladder or bowels are full, they empty their contents automatically.

Inside the controlled environment of the womb, the baby's temperature stayed slightly above the mother's body temperature. Now, the baby is exposed for the first time to fluctuating heat and cold. Because infants lose heat more rapidly than they can generate it at first, newborns usually are placed in a bassinet equipped with a radiant warmer to keep them comfortable during the adjustment period. Shortly after delivery, a nurse sometimes places a knit cap on the baby's head — the part of the body that loses heat most rapidly.

The aftermath of childbirth

When the delivery has proceeded normally, the obstetrician may present the newborn to her mother within moments after birth. If you are not feeling too exhausted, you may choose to hold your new baby for a few minutes while the final stage of childbirth — the delivery of the placenta — is completed.

If you are one of those mothers who feel up to nursing on the delivery table, there is a specific physiological benefit to be gained in doing so: The baby's sucking stimulates nerves in the breasts and causes the release of a hormone called oxytocin, which helps the uterus contract and minimizes post-delivery bleeding.

However, if your baby is premature, has a below-average birth weight for her fetal age or was delivered by cesarean section, the option to nurse on the delivery table may not be offered. In these cases, a baby is usually whisked away to the observation nursery first for a brief examination and special care.

Parents' first hurdles

If the baby faces some formidable challenges at birth, her parents are also adjusting to changes — many of them unexpected. Despite any prenatal training, you may have been unprepared for the powerful effects of the final contractions, or the baby may have presented herself to the birth canal in a way that made a last-minute cesarean section necessary.

Harder to prepare for, and even less predictable, are the emotions that can turn the birthing process into a roller-coaster ride. Feelings of joy and overwhelming love often mix with anxiety, confusion and even resentment. The new father may feel stirrings of jealousy as he looks upon this rival for his wife's attention and affection. If he has been present at the birth, he may be upset or disappointed if it did not proceed as he expected. As many as one in four new mothers even has the unsettling experience of looking upon her newborn as a stranger who does not really belong to her.

All such reactions are perfectly natural consequences of this great turning point in a couple's life, and in most cases they are quickly eclipsed by the exciting reality of having the long-awaited son or daughter at last.

Newborn intelligence

You will soon discover that your little one is remarkably well-equipped to learn about you and the big, new world he has entered. Until fairly recently, the newborn was viewed as a passive receptacle who experienced the world, in the words of the 19th-century psychologist William James, as one great "blooming, buzzing confusion." People generally believed that babies emerged from the womb with neither sight, hearing, taste, touch nor smell developed enough to take in any sensory information. And so, expecting little of their baby, the parents saw what they looked for.

But in recent years, a different picture has emerged. Modern researchers have found that the newborn arrives with an astonishing amount of sensory ability, that he is well equipped to signal many of his needs and that his brain is ready immediately to begin sorting, remembering and responding to sensations.

What babies see

Though his visual equipment is not yet matured — newborns have blurred vision and can see little beyond a distance of about 18 inches — the baby can see everything he needs for now, most notably the parent

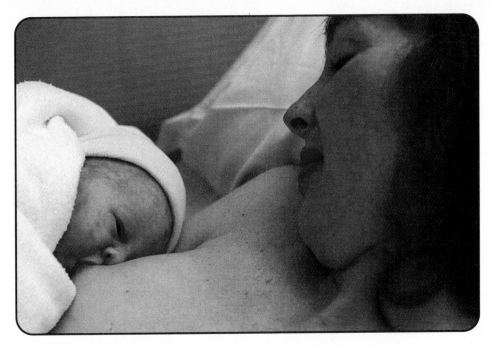

who holds him and the breast or bottle that provides his nourishment. Some researchers theorize that the baby's limited vision actually helps protect him against too much visual stimulation at this early stage, when his natural curiosity and eagerness to learn might otherwise overload his fledgling sensory system.

The newborn can also blink to shield his eyes from bright lights, and he soon has enough visual perception of potential danger to protect himself with a reflexive response, sometimes putting his hands between himself and any large object that approaches too close. The baby's eyes are sensitive to bright colors, such as red and yellow, and he can already detect contrasts between light and dark. He is selective in what he prefers to look at, showing more interest in human faces, patterns, sharp outlines and moving objects than in stationary objects, plain surfaces and solid forms.

The sense of hearing   Your baby is born with acute hearing and almost immediately can pick up a full range of sounds. Within 10 minutes of birth he may be able to associate sound with source and will turn his head in the appropriate direction. We know that he can discriminate between intensities of sound, as measured by increases in his heart rate that parallel increases in volume.

Sophisticated research techniques even suggest that a newborn may already have an ear for his mother's voice — possibly because he had been living with a muffled version of it for months in the womb. In one experiment, babies as young as three days old were tested for this subtle, discriminatory ability in the following way: Each infant, by sucking on a specially-rigged nipple, could turn on a recording of various women's voices, including that of his mother. The researchers found that more than 90 percent of the babies sucked harder when the voice they activated was that of their own mother. Coincidentally, perhaps, newborns also show a preference for higher-pitched voices.

Taste, smell and touch   The baby's senses of taste and smell are well developed at birth. He can discriminate between sweet and bitter immediately, with salt and sour soon following. Among these, only sweet — a taste associated with both mother's milk and commercial infant formulas — seems to hold any appeal for him. The newborn typically can identify his mother by smell, too, within five to 10 days after birth. The identification sometimes becomes so strong that he will refuse to drink from a supplemental bottle of formula from his mother — perhaps because it doesn't taste and smell like her milk — although the infant will accept the same bottle if someone else offers it.

The sense of touch is so acute that it becomes a key form of communication between the newborn and his parents. From the beginning, your baby responds to skin-to-skin contact, becoming calmer or more stimulated depending on the kind of touching he receives. He responds favorably to close cuddling — possibly because the sense of confinement reminds him of the coziness of the womb.

Styles of waking behavior

No matter how inherently active and responsive your newborn is, she will demonstrate sensory alertness only intermittently, during daily cyclical periods that neonatal specialists refer to as the "quiet alert" state. These periods take up about 10 percent of the infant's day; the rest of the time your baby is protected from overstimulation by a slowing of her responses.

You can recognize the times when your newborn is receptive and tuned in to her surroundings by the intense way in which she stares around her, eyes wide open and shining. Her body and face remain relatively inactive at these times, as though she is concentrating all her energies on absorbing and learning.

Some babies, particularly those who were delivered through natural or drug-free childbirth, enter the world in this state and remain alert for as long as 45 minutes. Researchers speculate that a surge of adrenaline, which accompanies the stress of birth, may account for this remarkable delivery-room behavior.

Quiet alert is just one of several distinct behavioral patterns your newborn goes through, in generally predictable sequence, several times a day. The "active alert" state, which often follows, is marked by slightly more physical movement and mild but continuous vocalization. Typically, this fussy stage is a signal that your newborn is beginning to feel hungry, tired or uncomfortable, or wants to be held. As the discomfort grows, her sounds graduate to outright crying, with a parallel intensification in physical movement.

The "crying state" usually comes to an end when the infant's hunger or discomfort is resolved — by feeding, falling asleep, passing a gas bubble or being picked up by a parent. Altogether, these three waking states fill about four to six hours of the newborn's day, though each incidence generally lasts no more than 20 minutes.

Sleep patterns

The rest of the time is devoted to alternating episodes of quiet sleep and active sleep. Your baby's quiet sleep is marked by eyes that are firmly closed and motionless, and little or no motor activity except for occa-

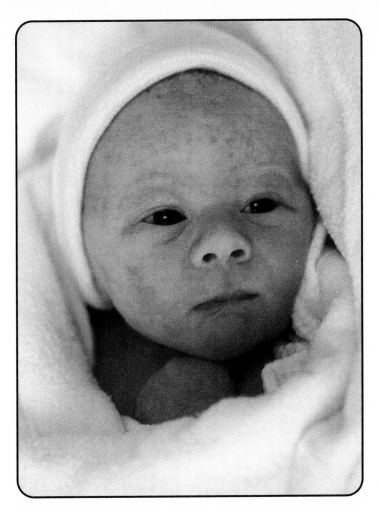

sional sucking or mouthing movements. She breathes deeply, with her abdomen rising and falling rhythmically, and seems impervious to noise around her.

Episodes of active sleep are somewhat lighter. They are marked by faster, more irregular breathing, some body activity and movement of the eyes beneath the closed lids. This state of sleep is comparable to the so-called rapid eye movement (REM), or dreaming, stage of sleep that adults experience, but no one knows whether the newborn experiences dreams. The newborn infant spends approximately half of her sleeping time in REM sleep, as opposed to 20 to 25 percent for the older baby and adult.

Quiet sleep and active sleep typically alternate at 30-minute intervals in sleep cycles lasting from three to four hours. In brief periods of drowsiness — a sixth state that often precedes or follows true sleep — you can notice that your infant breathes more shallowly than while sleeping, moves very little and wears a dazed expression as she looks out through half-closed eyes.

In many newborns, this pattern of waking and sleeping behavior runs fairly smoothly from birth, although it will change during the weeks and months ahead. In the meantime, learning and adjusting to your infant's individual cyclical patterns will make life easier for everyone during the hectic early days of her life. ❖

Portrait of a Newborn

In the eyes of their doting parents, newborn babies are awe-inspiring and uniquely beautiful creations. Their outer dimensions, however, are surprisingly similar: 95 percent weigh between five and a half and 10 pounds and measure between 18 and 22 inches in length. And for the first day or two, they may not look exactly like the dimpled cherubs their parents expected. Indeed, some parents may be taken aback by the initial appearance of their baby, with his enormous head, wrinkled skin and unsculpted face. This apprehension may be heightened by the flurry of activity as medical personnel subject the baby to a series of tests *(page 16)* and perhaps treat him for minor medical problems.

To be sure, even the healthiest newborn will need a few days to re-

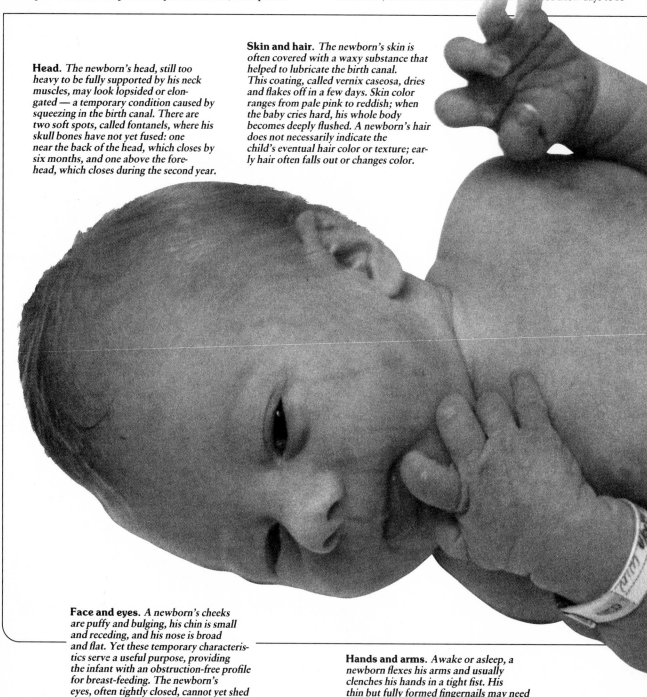

Head. *The newborn's head, still too heavy to be fully supported by his neck muscles, may look lopsided or elongated — a temporary condition caused by squeezing in the birth canal. There are two soft spots, called fontanels, where his skull bones have not yet fused: one near the back of the head, which closes by six months, and one above the forehead, which closes during the second year.*

Skin and hair. *The newborn's skin is often covered with a waxy substance that helped to lubricate the birth canal. This coating, called vernix caseosa, dries and flakes off in a few days. Skin color ranges from pale pink to reddish; when the baby cries hard, his whole body becomes deeply flushed. A newborn's hair does not necessarily indicate the child's eventual hair color or texture; early hair often falls out or changes color.*

Face and eyes. *A newborn's cheeks are puffy and bulging, his chin is small and receding, and his nose is broad and flat. Yet these temporary characteristics serve a useful purpose, providing the infant with an obstruction-free profile for breast-feeding. The newborn's eyes, often tightly closed, cannot yet shed tears; tear glands are not fully functional until a month after birth. His initial eye color may change as he grows.*

Hands and arms. *Awake or asleep, a newborn flexes his arms and usually clenches his hands in a tight fist. His thin but fully formed fingernails may need trimming to prevent facial scratches.*

cover from the squeezing and pushing his body has just endured. Initially, he may lose up to half a pound in weight as moisture evaporates from his body tissues and his digestive processes struggle to adapt. Yet in as short a time as one week, he will have regained the lost weight and begun a spurt of growth that will double his birth weight in only five months.

Parents may also view their baby's body parts as unsynchronized and out of proportion. His head, which will measure only one eighth of his height by adulthood, now accounts for a full quarter of his length. But the disproportion is not without reason: The newborn's head must be this sizable to accommodate his relatively large brain, which has already reached one third of its adult dimensions.

Torso. *With narrow hips and a chest that is smaller in circumference than the head, the newborn's torso appears oddly out of proportion. In the first days of life, his protruding abdomen is dominated by the stump of the umbilical cord, seen here clamped at birth to halt bleeding. The stump dries up and falls off by itself within a week or two.*

Legs and feet. *The newborn's legs, usually flexed against the abdomen, appear bowed and short. His feet look flat because of protective fat on the soles, and they have pliable cartilage instead of bones, except for the heel. His still-developing circulatory system often leaves his toes blue and cold.*

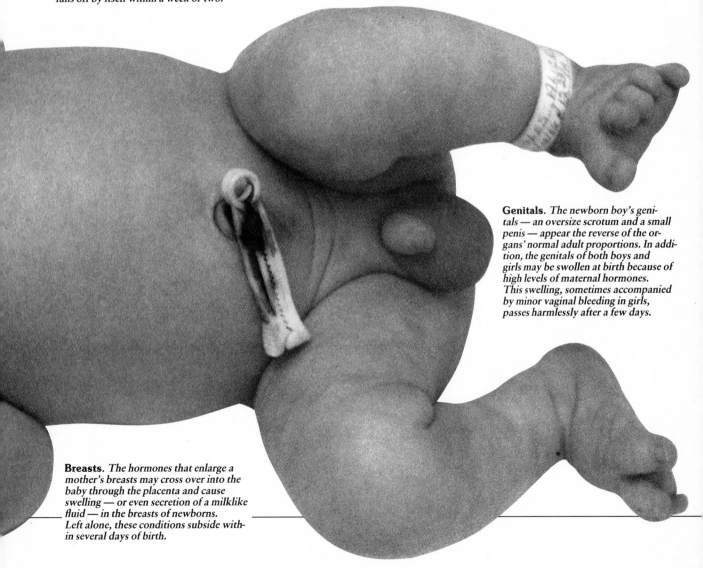

Genitals. *The newborn boy's genitals — an oversize scrotum and a small penis — appear the reverse of the organs' normal adult proportions. In addition, the genitals of both boys and girls may be swollen at birth because of high levels of maternal hormones. This swelling, sometimes accompanied by minor vaginal bleeding in girls, passes harmlessly after a few days.*

Breasts. *The hormones that enlarge a mother's breasts may cross over into the baby through the placenta and cause swelling — or even secretion of a milklike fluid — in the breasts of newborns. Left alone, these conditions subside within several days of birth.*

Screening Tests to Detect Early Problems

The first 24 hours of life are critical in determining how well a newborn will adjust to the world outside the womb. Obstetricians routinely perform a series of tests — among them the ones below — to minimize the possibility of any serious problems. In some cases, a doctor's prompt decision based on test results can prevent complications that, if untreated, could result in irreversible defects.

The obstetrician is responsible for the newborn's immediate care. As the infant's breathing is checked and her umbilical cord clamped, usually within the first minute of life, a nurse records the time of birth and any obvious abnormalities. The newborn is then given her first important test, the Apgar, which rates the strength of her vital functions. If there are no complications, she is dried, wrapped up and given a more detailed physical examination.

Blood samples for tests are taken when the umbilical cord is cut or they are drawn with gentle pinpricks from the baby's heel. The newborn receives a vitamin K injection to normalize clotting in her immature circulatory system, and an antibiotic or drops of silver nitrate are placed in her eyes to prevent the development of any infection contracted in the birth canal. The newborn's footprints are then recorded and a name tag is fastened to her ankle or wrist.

Apgar. This universally accepted test measures five newborn vital signs: heart rate, breathing, muscle activity, reflexes and skin color. It is given exactly one minute after birth and again four minutes later. Each of the five categories is assigned a maximum of two points, with 10 being the highest overall score. In scoring skin color, for example, a newborn with blue skin would get a zero. A baby with a pink trunk and blue limbs would score one, and an all-pink body, two. A low initial score is not necessarily cause for alarm; however, babies with initial scores of three or below require immediate resuscitation. Healthy newborns should score close to 10 after five minutes.

Delivery room exam. Once a doctor or nurse determines that the newborn has no immediate problems, a more thorough physical examination is conducted. The baby is checked for major abnormalities, bruises and limb movement. Since premature babies require special nursery care, the newborn's gestational age — time spent in the womb — is also estimated.

Nursery appraisal. After spending some time with her mother, the newborn is moved to the nursery, where she is measured, weighed and closely observed for several hours as she sleeps in a heated crib. Her temperature and breathing are monitored, and her umbilical cord is checked to make sure it is dry and healing. The umbilical clamp is left on for at least 24 hours; an anti-septic ointment may be applied to prevent infection. To check for congenital problems with the newborn's urinary system and bowels, nurses make sure that urine and stool are passed within the first 24 hours.

Pediatrician's checkup. Within 24 hours of the baby's birth, your pediatrician or family doctor will typically conduct his own examination at the hospital. He will evaluate the baby's heart, reflexes, joints and general alertness, and gently probe her abdomen to check internal organs. He may repeat this examination just before the baby and mother are discharged from the hospital. Parents often attend this examination, which provides a good opportunity to discuss feeding, sleeping, circumcision *(page 20)* and other questions.

PKU. Between the second and sixth days of life, a blood sample from the newborn's heel is screened for PKU, or phenylketonuria, a rare disorder that prevents the breakdown of amino acids found in milk and meat products. While this condition affects only about one in every 14,000 newborns, it can cause brain damage unless detected early and treated with a stringent diet.

Hypothyroidism. A blood sample is also screened for hypothyroidism, a hormone deficiency that affects one in every 4,000 newborns. Sufficient thyroid hormones are critical during a baby's first five months, when the brain cells are developing most rapidly. Left untreated, hypothyroidism can cause mental retardation and stunted growth; if detected early, it can be corrected with replacement hormones.

Coombs test. Performed on blood taken from the umbilical cord, this routine test screens for an antibody that indicates a blood incompatibility between mother and baby. While a positive result does not necessarily mean the baby is in danger, it alerts doctors to watch for common complications, such as severe jaundice.

Blood-sugar level. Newborns with low blood-sugar levels, or hypoglycemia, are prone to restlessness and irritability and, in very severe cases, seizures or mental retardation. Screening, which is conducted only on newborns in high-risk categories — such as children of diabetic mothers — involves testing blood from the baby's heel. Low blood-sugar can be readily treated with frequent feedings or, if necessary, with intravenous solutions of glucose and water.

Brazelton test. With their parents' permission, some newborns may be given a behavioral test designed to assess their capabilities in such areas as adaptability, alertness and response to being cuddled. The test rates an infant's response to 25 activities involving colors, shapes, bells, rattles, lights and other stimuli. The tests, usually performed over several days, are used as research tools in the study of newborn behavior.

Medical Conditions Common in Newborns

Considering what they have been through, it is remarkable that most newborns — nearly 90 percent — arrive in healthy condition. There are, however, several temporary conditions that frequently develop during the first month, and it is only natural for parents to fret about anything that looks unusual. Many newborns have rashes, puffy eyes, yellowish skin or bruises — conditions that usually disappear on their own. Feel free to ask your doctor about anything that worries you or any condition that persists. Bear in mind that most congenital discolorations and bruises clear up on their own — even some birthmarks. At some point in the first month, most newborns exhibit one or more of the reversible conditions described below.

Jaundice. For the first week of life, a newborn's still immature liver has trouble breaking down a yellow substance called bilirubin, a by-product of the fetus's extra red blood cells. As a result, 70 percent of newborns develop a yellowish skin color during the first days after birth. This yellow tinge, or jaundice, normally disappears in seven to 14 days, when the liver begins working efficiently. If the jaundice persists or worsens beyond the first week, or if the baby develops jaundice due to incompatibility with his mother's blood type, prompt treatment may be called for. Some jaundice is treated by exposing the baby to the bilirubin-reducing rays of a special lamp. More severe cases, resulting from incompatibilities, may require blood exchange transfusions.

Rashes. Newborns may have a number of rashes that are generally harmless and disappear on their own. Small white spots called milia, caused by blocked ducts, may appear around the nose. Newborns may also suffer from acne-like rashes, caused by maternal hormones, and they may develop blotchy red spots with raised white or yellow centers, resembling heat rash. Like milia, these require no special treatment.

Birthmarks. Caused by extra blood vessels or pigment deposits, birthmarks in a wide range of shapes and colors are quite common in newborns. Many babies have blotchy pink or purple marks, known as stork bites, at the back of their necks or on their eyelids; these often fade during the first year. One in 10 newborns has a strawberry mark. These raised red lesions appear after birth, grow rapidly for one to two years and generally fade by a child's seventh year. Only three of every 1,000 newborns have port-wine stains, unraised purple marks that may cover a large area and normally require cosmetic treatment. Twenty percent of newborns have café-au-lait marks, coffee-colored discolorations that can be distinguished from moles — which are raised — by their flat profile. Most dark-skinned babies are born with blue-gray, bruiselike marks near the base of the spine. Known as Mongolian spots, these marks have no connection with Down syndrome, which used to be called mongolism, and disappear within several years.

Delivery marks. Elongated, reddish marks on the baby's cheeks or forehead, caused by the obstetrician's forceps, and small purple bruises, caused by blood vessels ruptured during delivery, normally disappear after a few days.

Body hair. The necks and shoulders of newborns are often covered with a soft, downy hair called lanugo. This fuzzy coating helps protect the baby's skin in the womb and is partially present at birth, especially in premature infants. Lanugo disappears by itself during the first few weeks.

Eye irritation. Birth pressure may cause tiny blood vessels in a newborn's eye to burst and may also cause a puffiness around the eyes. Both conditions disappear by themselves in a few days. The eye ointment or drops given to babies to prevent infection may sometimes cause a temporary yellow discharge from the eyes. If the discharge persists, then your pediatrician may recommend using a washing solution.

Cross-eyes. Newborns often have crossed or wandering eyes because the muscles that control their eye movements are not yet coordinated. If a baby's eyes are crossed all the time, or if the appearance persists for several months, then the child should be examined by an eye specialist.

Mouth problems. In the first few weeks after birth, some babies develop a mouth infection known as thrush. Caused by a fungus that may be transmitted by unwashed hands and unsterilized bottles, thrush looks like a white coating of cottage cheese. The infection can be treated with antifungal medication to prevent it from spreading to the mother during breast-feeding.

Vigorous sucking on bottles and pacifiers may cause newborns to develop blisters on the upper lip. Harmless white cysts called Epstein's pearls, may also appear on the palate or gums. Both conditions are noninfectious and disappear on their own.

Cradle cap. Newborns commonly suffer from flaky, peeling scalps, a condition called cradle cap. Its dandruff-like symptoms can be treated with baby oil or with special shampoo.

Protruding navel. A weakness in the newborn's abdominal muscle wall may result in an umbilical hernia, a painless swelling near the navel. Although these hernias cause some parents considerable concern, they should not be compressed or strapped down in any manner. Most heal within a year's time without special treatment.

Bowel problems. Before a newborn makes his first normal bowel movement, the greenish black substance called meconium that filled his intestines in the womb must be eliminated. If this does not occur within 24 hours, the nursery staff will alert the doctor. The baby's first stools may also contain traces of blood that the baby ingested during the delivery. No treatment is necessary.

Hiccuping and sneezing. Although frequent hiccuping may cause a newborn to spit up, it is normal in newborns and no cause for concern. Nursing or giving the infant warm water may help to halt the hiccups. Sneezing is also normal, since it is the only way a newborn can blow his nose. If the infant is congested, gently suction his nose with a bulb syringe, or tickle his nose with cotton to help make him sneeze.

Natal teeth. Occasionally a baby is born with a tooth already in place, usually a lower incisor. A healthy tooth need not be extracted, but if an X-ray reveals that the tooth is loose and has weak roots, removal may be recommended to prevent swallowing it during feeding.

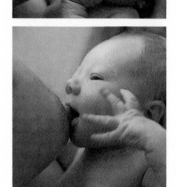

A Baby's Built-In Reflexes

Despite their apparent helplessness, newborns come into the world equipped with a wide array of survival tools. They quiver and cry to communicate their needs, and they cough and sneeze to clear their respiratory passages. They know instinctively how to suck and swallow once they latch onto a nipple.

These reactions, known as reflexes, are inborn and involuntary responses that form part of a complex interaction between mother and child. The newborn's crying or searching for a breast evokes maternal responses, such as cuddling and nursing, that the infant needs in order to live. At the same time, the mutually reinforcing cycle of reflex and response helps the mother properly fulfill her role as nurturer. Since these reflexes are present in all normal newborns and last for predictable periods, your baby's responses serve as early indicators of nervous-system functioning and physical coordination.

In a comprehensive examination, medical personnel will attempt to elicit the responses shown at right and below, watching carefully for an absent or asymmetrical reflex. Some of the reflexes are clearly survival tools, such as the rooting reflex that enables the newborn to nurse. But others, such as the Babkin reflex, serve no obvious purpose. Still others, like the grasping and startle reflexes, may be vestiges of our simian ancestry — responses that help a baby monkey cling to its mother and grasp a branch during a fall. But this is purely speculation.

You may want to ask to be present during these tests or you may want to evoke some of the responses — such as the rooting or Babkin reflexes — on your own. But testing other reflexes, such as the startle or the grasping, requires a carefully controlled manipulation of the newborn's head or body that is best left to professionals. In addition, only trained personnel can accurately interpret your child's responses, which may vary depending on such factors as alertness and hunger.

Babinski reflex. *When the sole is stroked from the heel up, the toes flare upward. After 12 to 18 months, the normal response is for the toes to curl downward.*

Rooting reflex. *When a newborn's cheek is gently stroked (top), he will turn his face toward the stimulus and open his mouth (above), searching for a nipple. This instinctive reaction enables the newborn to use his sense of touch to find nourishment while his senses of sight and smell are still developing.*

Startle reflex. *If a newborn's equilibrium is suddenly disturbed — by letting his head drop back a few inches, for example — he responds by kicking his legs, flinging his arms upward with hands outstretched and then pulling back his arms, fists clenched, toward his chest. This burst of activity, which is known as the Moro or startle reflex, can also be elicited by sudden or loud noises.*

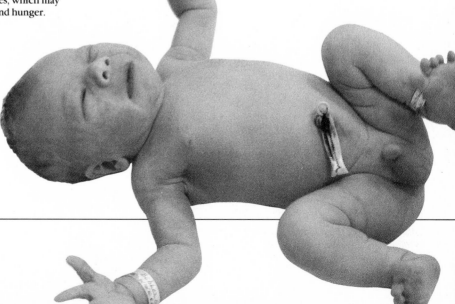

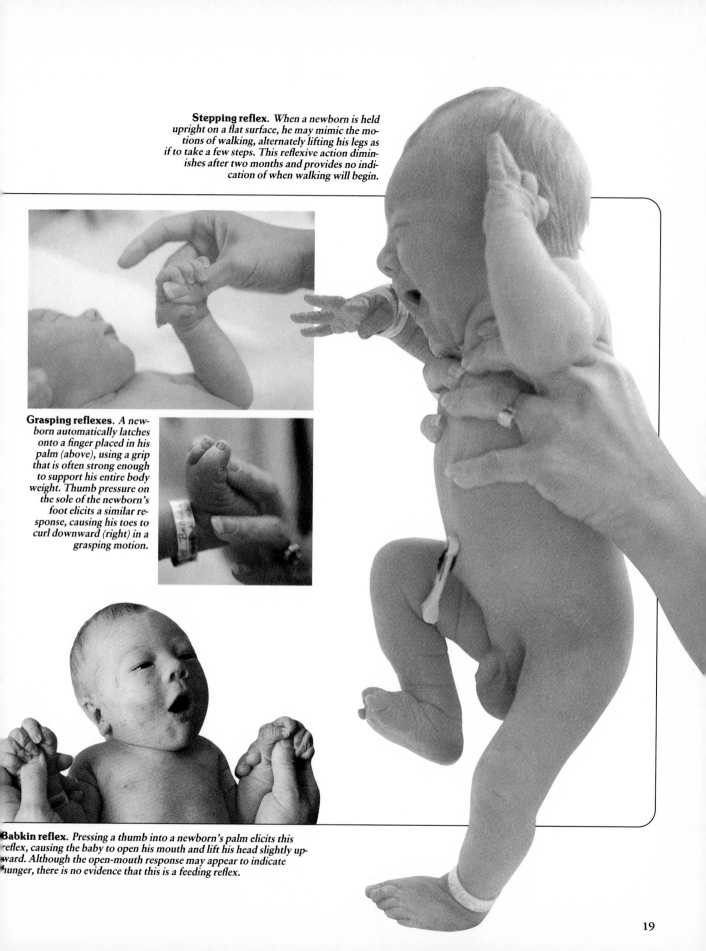

Stepping reflex. *When a newborn is held upright on a flat surface, he may mimic the motions of walking, alternately lifting his legs as if to take a few steps. This reflexive action diminishes after two months and provides no indication of when walking will begin.*

Grasping reflexes. *A newborn automatically latches onto a finger placed in his palm (above), using a grip that is often strong enough to support his entire body weight. Thumb pressure on the sole of the newborn's foot elicits a similar response, causing his toes to curl downward (right) in a grasping motion.*

Babkin reflex. *Pressing a thumb into a newborn's palm elicits this reflex, causing the baby to open his mouth and lift his head slightly upward. Although the open-mouth response may appear to indicate hunger, there is no evidence that this is a feeding reflex.*

19

Your Hospital Stay

Usually about an hour after delivery, mother and child are taken off to the rooms where they will spend the next few days recovering and being monitored. Hospital accommodations for post partum patients vary greatly, so you should investigate your options well ahead of time with your obstetrician to ensure the best choice for you and your family. Some hospitals offer rooming in, which allows a newborn to remain in the same room with his mother for the entire stay. Other hospitals favor a modified version in which you keep your baby with you throughout the day. During nighttime hours, he is taken off to the maternity nursery. All institutions provide, as well, the kinds of accommodations that your mother and grandmother probably knew when they gave birth: a private or semiprivate room for you and full-time nursery care for your baby.

Rooming in Keeping the newborn in your room is a natural extension of today's prepared-birth experience and, consequently, is becoming increasingly popular. The arrangement offers you an extended opportunity to get to know your new infant before you take him home, a kind of dress rehearsal for all concerned. In particular, you have a chance to handle, change and bathe your baby repeatedly, under the guidance of the nursing staff, and to ask questions as they arise. Having him close by in all his moods and in all his states of waking and sleeping will help you begin to form a sense of your child as a real person. You become accustomed to his breathing, to his unfamiliar gurgles and grunts. You listen to his cries and begin to make some sense of how he expresses and communicates his various discomforts. And the two of you begin to relax with one another.

Visitor rules are generally more flexible for rooming-in units. Fathers may come at any time and are encouraged to handle the baby and to care for him, with the proviso that they observe hospital hygiene practices such as hand-scrubbing and wearing a hospital gown.

Nursery care Many women, especially those with a toddler or two at home, prefer to rest during the two or three days following delivery. If you are one of them, then the private or semiprivate room is the sensible choice. Nurses will care for your newborn around the clock, except during daytime feedings, when he is brought to you all sweet-smelling and neat. Feeding visits work out to about 30 minutes in each four-hour period. This is hardly enough time to become fast friends, but — as proponents of nursery care point out — there is an equally important advantage: You will be addressing your own physical and psychological needs, which is essential if you are going to meet your baby's demands adequately in the weeks and months ahead.

The hospital day Whatever accommodations you choose, you will find that the daily routine on the maternity floor varies little from other parts of the hospital. The day starts very early, since nurses have a great deal to do before the doctors make their morning rounds: Babies must be changed, every-

The Choice of Circumcision

In American hospitals, parents of newborn boys are usually offered the option of circumcision, the surgical removal of the flap of foreskin from the head of the penis. The simple operation is normally performed by a physician before the mother and baby leave the hospital. Although the procedure is uncommon in other Western nations, 80 percent of baby boys born in the U.S. are currently being circumcised.

In recent years, however, the widespread procedure has become controversial. Circumcision was long believed to reduce the risk of venereal disease and cancer, but the American Academy of Pediatrics now maintains that routine circumcision has no proven medical benefits. Parents who decide to have their sons circumcised usually do so because of social or religious custom or for reasons relating to personal hygiene.

one's temperature must be taken, and all must be fed. Throughout the day, interruptions are frequent, as hospital personnel check the new mother's pulse, respiration, blood pressure and the condition of her abdomen, uterus and perineum.

In addition, you may have baby-care classes to go to, exercises to do, thank-you notes to write and family and friends to greet — while your telephone rings constantly with congratulatory calls. At times, the nicest thing that you can think of is for everyone to just go away and leave you in peace.

Time to adjust   Such feelings are very natural among post partum mothers and if you need time alone, by all means, arrange for it. See only close family if you wish, and do not be afraid to let them know that 15 minutes or so is about your limit right now. Have your telephone calls held and hang a Do Not Disturb sign on your closed door for an hour or two during the afternoon to give you time to catch up with yourself. If your baby is being cared for in the nursery, you can even ask that she be bottle-fed at the next feeding.

Nothing now is more important than the restoration of your energy and well-being. A new mother's body is going through tumultuous changes: Conditions that were nine months in the making are being reversed or altered. The heart and kidneys, digestive, urinary and reproductive systems — all of these are readjusting to life without the fetus, and these changes are bound to take their toll on the mother. Even more profound are the fast-paced hormonal changes that occur as the new mother prepares to lactate.

Early nursing

The onset of lactation, which is the production of true milk, normally occurs three to four days after delivery. It is brought on by large decreases in the production of the hormones progesterone and estrogen, a natural result of the detachment of the placenta. If you choose not to breast-feed — something you have presumably discussed and resolved with your obstetrician and pediatrician well before the birth — then you probably will be given small doses of progesterone and estrogen, together with a third hormone, androgen, to suppress lactation at this time. Otherwise, your breasts begin to enlarge and engorge now, the skin becomes shiny and taut, and a certain amount of discomfort occurs as your system adjusts.

The value of colostrum

Whichever way you go for the long term, you will want to give serious consideration to nursing in the brief period before true milk starts flowing. Your breasts at this time are filled with colostrum, a colorless to pale yellowish fluid that is the ideal starter food for all babies. Because it is higher in protein and lower in carbohydrates and fats than breast milk or formula, it is more easily digested by the newborn. At the same time, colostrum has a mildly laxative effect, which helps to flush meconium, the greenish black fecal material that accumulates in a baby's digestive tract prior to birth. More significantly, colostrum confers on your baby temporary immunity to such infectious agents as the polio virus, the staphylococcus and Escherichia coli bacteria, and any other microorganisms to which you have acquired an immunity over the years. Your gift of immunity will last only as long as you continue to breast-feed.

When bonding begins

Sharing your colostrum with your baby is also a natural and unselfconscious way to initiate the communication that will gradually deepen into bonds of attachment between mother and child. Numerous studies have been made — and volumes written — about the magical love-tie known as bonding. Perhaps the most important thing new parents should know about this phenomenon is that it is not an automatic or instantaneous tie that binds, but rather a gradual weaving together of personalities. Like the growth of love between husband and wife, this attachment will continue to evolve over the years, changing as mother, father and child develop in each other's company.

Parents who can begin the process of bonding in the hospital certainly have a good head start toward enjoying the most profound pleasures of parenthood, but those who feel no such emotions at the time of delivery, or even in the first days or weeks of their baby's life, should not be concerned that they can never catch up. Many factors will contribute ultimately to this attachment: the parents' own childhood experiences and family customs, the relationship between the husband and wife, how the pregnancy and delivery went, the physical condition of mother and child immediately after birth, and not least, the inborn temperaments of everyone involved. In short, the bonding experience is one that simply cannot be rushed or forced. Most mothers and fathers find that it happens quite naturally and spontaneously as they attend to the multitude of concrete, practical challenges facing them at this turning point in their lives.

Before heading home If you are like most new mothers, you will stay in the hospital only two or three days before going home with your baby to cope with all the challenges on your own. While you still can, take advantage of the professional counsel available to you in the hospital. Be sure the obstetrician takes time to check you thoroughly before you leave. If you had an episiotomy or cesarean section, find out what to expect regarding healing and how to handle your own comfort and cleanliness. While you are at it, get your physician's explicit advice regarding the resumption of sexual relations and of appropriate birth-control methods. Try to have your partner present, or discuss the subject with him ahead of time so that you can pass on his concerns.

Hemorrhoids and constipation frequently accompany childbirth, but both can be managed if you get good advice and the proper medication. Discuss such issues with the doctor or nurse, and do not leave the hospital until you can move your bowels successfully. Find out how much and what kind of exercises you should do daily. If you have back pain, which is not uncommon after delivery, ask for suggestions on minimizing the strain.

Breast-feeding mothers need special advice regarding maternal nutrition: As many as 1,000 of your daily calories will be diverted to the baby's nourishment. You should also be prepared for possible difficulty in producing milk in the beginning and for some breast discomfort along the way. An obstetric nurse can advise you on these and other breast-feeding matters.

Finally, check with your pediatrician or a pediatric nurse about the baby's feeding needs and bowel movements, the healing of the umbilical cord, the care of the circumcised penis and other newborn-care concerns. Learning what you should expect ahead of time will help prepare you to handle such matters with confidence when you meet them head on at home. ⁘

A Well-Prepared Homecoming

The transition from hospital to home will go more smoothly if arrangements have been thought out in advance. This check list leaves little to chance:

- Get an appropriate car seat for the baby and use it on the ride home.

- Pack a going-home tote with diapers, a clean change of clothes for the baby, bottles of formula if you are not nursing and a small notebook for last-minute instructions.

- Dress yourself in something that is comfortable for your present shape.

Although you may have lost a dozen pounds or more since giving birth, it will take some time for your abdomen to trim down.

- Before leaving the hospital, ask your pediatrician or pediatric nurse any lingering questions about such ordinary eventualities as hiccups, diarrhea, fussiness and diaper rash.

- If you are bottle-feeding your newborn, double-check instructions for sterilizing and preparing formula.

- Have a nursery area waiting at home

where the baby will be comfortable and close to you. Include a place to sleep and equipment for feeding, changing and bathing.

- Make sure your home supply of diapers is sufficient to see the baby through the first few days. A newborn will use about 100 diapers a week. You should also have a minimum newborn wardrobe (page 46).

- Arrange to go home to a quiet house with no guests. Celebratory parties can wait until you and the baby have adjusted to your new life.

The New Family at Home

As you enter your front door with the baby, elation may well be mixed with heavy doses of anxiety and exhaustion. Here, cradled in your arms, is a new little being — at once helpless in his ability to care for himself and all-powerful in his claims on you and your partner. There are several ways you can prepare in advance to cope with the stresses of the newborn days — beginning with a simple acceptance of the changed family dynamics, and a reordering of priorities that puts the welfare of mother and child at the top of the list *(box, page 31)*.

Help from outside

One of the best ways to lessen the strain of caring for a newborn is to have someone come in to help for a week or two. Your mother, mother-in-law or a sister may first come to mind, but there are circumstances in which a temporary housekeeper or baby nurse would be the better choice. With a relative, personal chemistry must be considered carefully. Ask yourselves if the candidate is fairly relaxed and nonjudgmental. Is she likely to follow your agenda, or will she have her own routines and expectations? If you have serious doubts in this area, you will be better off avoiding the problem from the start rather than having to persuade a loved one to go home early.

Budget permitting, the wisest course often is to hire a temporary helper, one who comes in for three or four hours a day. She will take over the kinds of chores that new mothers least want and least need to do — such as making meals, doing dishes, washing clothes, straightening and cleaning the house — leaving you free to spend your limited energies caring for your new baby.

Introducing the baby

A new baby is a big event in almost everybody's book, and you should be prepared for everyone from your next-door neighbor to the postman to drop by for a look as soon as you arrive home. When and how you introduce the baby to others is strictly up to you. Some mothers thrive on all the attention, while others prefer to postpone entertaining for a while. In any case, try to keep visits these first few days to a minimum and schedule them for a time of day when you and your baby feel best.

One problem you should be legitimately concerned about is protecting your baby from infection and overstimulation. Politely ask people with colds to stay away, and keep the handling and fussing to a

minimum. If you feel awkward about saying no, blame the rules on your pediatrician.

Sibling rivalry If you have an older child, introducing him to his new sibling will take top priority, if he has not already met the baby during a hospital visit. When you first get home, it is a good idea to have the father hang back for a few moments with the baby while you enjoy a brief, exclusive reunion with the older child. After the baby makes her entrance, let her big brother examine her, if he wants to, or even sit securely on the sofa and hold her, if he is old enough.

When the initial novelty has worn off, be prepared for some fairly predictable behavior to set in. From a toddler's point of view, the newcomer has stolen the limelight with ease. Some jealousy and resentment are inevitable.

To reassure your older child, devote as much time as you can to him during these days, preferably while the baby naps. Ask visitors to bring him a gift, however inexpensive, when they come to call on the new baby. Most important, anticipate — and up to a point, make allowances for — disruptive behavior on the part of your older child. It will take him some time to develop the big-brother spirit.

Pets and the baby The dog or cat that has long had the run of your house and your affection may also feel jealous when a new baby suddenly becomes No. 1. If you have a rambunctious or high-strung dog, spend a few sessions with it at obedience-training school before your baby is due. As a minimum goal, train it to sit and stay on command and to refrain from jumping up on hind legs when excited. When the baby comes home, make the initial introduction a careful one and watch your dog closely.

Cats and kittens should be introduced with care, too, although cats are generally not as large or as interested in the child as dogs. And despite the wives' tales, they will not suck breath out of an unattended infant and suffocate her. Nevertheless, you should not leave the baby and a cat — or any pet — alone together until they are on comfortable terms with each other.

A baby's physical changes

Your baby, like you, is doing her best to adjust. In the hospital she became accustomed to one environment. Now a whole new range of sensations washes around her, and a number of internal changes are taking place. She is beginning a growth spurt, regaining ounces lost in the first hours after delivery; if she is typical, around the 10th day she will reach and surpass her original birth weight. Her nervous system expands rapidly as millions of neural connections are made for the first time. Organs become more competent, muscles firmer. Her eyes focus faster and more precisely every day.

With so many things happening, even a generally placid baby is likely to be agitated and fussy for a while. She may eat poorly and erratically, doze fitfully and wake feeling fatigued, breathe irregularly at times and thrash about with no apparent reason. She is likely to sneeze, hiccup, gag, spit up and startle frequently. This behavior is a normal part of the incredible development a newborn undergoes in the first weeks of life.

Why newborns cry

Another response you can count on is your baby's cry. Crying is a newborn's primary means of communication, a compelling signal that she needs to be fed, changed or simply held and comforted. Depending on her temperament, your baby may cry in stretches lasting a few minutes or an hour; in any event, if she is typical, crying and fussing will occupy a significant part of her waking life at first.

There are many ways you can try to soothe a crying infant *(pages 48-51)*, but much of the newborn's agitation must simply be taken in stride. Some doctors theorize that crying and fussing at this stage represent a discharging of physiological tensions, which may be necessary for babies to move on developmentally. Crying has also been recognized as one way an infant shuts out the overwhelming stimuli around her.

At these times, the best solution for both of you is probably to pick up your baby and cuddle her closely. Studies of parenting styles in many cultures have shown that the more quickly and consistently a baby's needs are met in infancy, the greater the child's security and independence will be later on. Many experts say flatly that it is impossible to spoil a baby with attention in the first year of life, and that parents should respond quickly to their baby's cry, whatever the cause.

An emerging schedule

If you observe your child closely, you will see certain patterns begin to emerge in her sleeping and waking behavior, although individual differences among newborns can be enormous. Babies at this stage sleep anywhere from 11 to 21 hours a day — 14 to 18 hours as an average. Feeding patterns also vary widely: Your baby may be content to be fed every five hours, or she may demand milk every two and a half hours — and still seem unsatisfied.

One trend you will be relieved to see is the gradual change-over from the fitful sleep patterns of the baby in her early days to the more settled and predictable slumber of the older baby. Newborns switch frequently between the REM and quiet sleep states *(page 12)* and are sometimes disturbed during transitions between the two types of sleep. They tend

Parent to Parent

Adjusting to Life with Baby

66 Friends can be too much of a good thing at the very beginning. We learned this by being 'too much' ourselves when our best friends had a baby. We were on their doorstep with a bottle of champagne when Paul and Sally came home from the hospital and we sat around celebrating, behaving as though this baby was a wonderful new pet. Meanwhile, the baby began to howl and Sally became more and more anxious. She took him upstairs but we continued to talk and laugh with Paul. It wasn't until Sally's mother interrupted to tell us to 'go home for heaven's sake' that we realized how thoughtless we had been. When our time came, we had no qualms about sending people away when we needed to be alone. 99

66 Motherhood seemed so unrelenting. And at the same time my husband was making his own demands. He comes from a family where women cater to their men. He didn't mean to be hard on me; he just was unaware of what was going on. He figured I was sitting around watching this nice baby with lots of time on my hands. So there we'd be with a less-than-fabulous meal on the table and the

baby would cry. My impulse was to jump up and feed the baby, and then my husband would say 'Are we going to have a normal life or are we going to have this child dictate to us?' Sometimes I wonder how we ever made it! 99

66 I worried a lot about visitors and germs, but I didn't have the courage to say 'Stay home.' I remember one time when my friend showed up and she said that her five-year-old and six-year-old had colds, but that they would stay outside. Well, it was winter, and I couldn't let these sniffly kids stand outside in the cold, so I invited them in. Thinking back, I realize my friend was putting me on the spot. I should have had the sense to suggest they come back a few days later. But I think new mothers sometimes do what they do because they need approval: You've gone through this long arduous thing and you need a lot of recognition and approval. 99

66 I expected that being home with the baby would be like a vacation. I imagined myself lying on the couch eating bonbons and reading all the Victorian novels I had always wanted to read. Was I ever shocked! My child was colicky, cried all the time and hardly ever napped.

I bottled up the frustration and once hit the couch so hard that I hurt my wrist. It sounds awful, but I came to understand how a parent can lose control and abuse her child. All these greeting cards and magazines that depict children as so angelic — they're doing us a disservice. We need permission to express negative feelings once in a while or we run the risk of exploding. 99

66 You do have to make time for yourself — and maintain a sense of humor. I learned that the hard way, after running myself down trying to be a perfect mother and homemaker. Finally, I said to myself, 'You don't have to prove anything to anyone. Get your priorities straight and stick to them. People before things.' I stopped dusting and cleaning and trying to make gourmet meals when James slept, and I tried sitting down and reading or napping instead. I found that just enjoying him, watching him grow and finding the humor in the chaos around me was best for all of us. 99

to take many short cat naps at first, without regard for day or night. As the weeks go on, however, your baby's sleeping time will become consolidated in longer stretches of sounder sleep.

Post partum reactions   Emotions new and old complicate the adjustments you are making during this period. An estimated 80 to 90 percent of new mothers feel some degree of post partum blues at any time up to six months after giving birth. The causes appear to be both physical and emotional. Gratified as the new mother is at having her baby at last, she now must deal with postoperative pain and physical exhaustion. Her uterus is returning from the two-pound organ it became during pregnancy to its normal two-ounce size. The outworn uterine lining is being shed and replaced by a new one. Stretched abdominal and lower-back muscles are gradually tightening, and breasts are swollen and tender.

Moreover, hormonal changes provoked by the birthing process create dramatic mood swings, which occur at the same time the new mother is shortchanged on sleep, especially on the deeper, dreaming stage of sleep that has the most restorative effects. And to top it all off, the intense maternal instinct that she had imagined would appear instantly may as yet be nowhere in sight. Motherhood at times seems not just an anticlimax, but a full-fledged disaster.

For the majority of women assaulted by such feelings, the post partum reaction is mild, relatively quick to pass and without long-term consequences. Popularly called the "baby blues," it usually shows up within a week after delivery. Typical reactions include irritability, difficulty in sleeping and concentrating, depressed appetite, a tendency to burst into tears over the most minor issues and generally feeling down. These symptoms usually disappear as mysteriously as they came. About one out of 10 new mothers experiences more serious and extended depression and may need professional counseling.

Taking the blues in stride

The best defense against post partum blues is to go on the counterattack. Sleep whenever you can, letting the baby's quiet times be your signal to relax. If you are nursing, try keeping the baby alongside you so that even if she awakens and wants a feeding you can continue to rest. Whether you are nursing or not, you will need to drink plenty of beverages daily to restore your normal fluid balance — eight to 12 glasses of water, juice and other liquids are recommended.

Exercise can do wonders for both body and spirit. Ask your doctor to recommend an appropriate bending and stretching routine that you can do at home, and get outside to walk or ride as soon as you are physically able. Even very new babies can take to the outdoors safely in all but the most extreme weather, and you will find the fresh air and activity restorative. If you live near a playground where mothers congregate, by all means join them. Almost everyone you meet will have a story to tell about how she weathered the baby blues.

And stay close, physically and emotionally, to your mate, who may be feeling some of the same lows you are experiencing. Studies have revealed that nearly two out of three new fathers experience their own version of the baby blues after birth. Its origin is not hormonal, obviously, but anxiety and lost sleep can take a heavy toll nonetheless.

The parents' changing relationship

One reality that will be unmistakably clear is the fact that life is significantly different and more complicated now than it was before the baby arrived. Your ability to accept from the start the changes that parenthood imposes — with pleasure rather than regret — will set the tone of your family life for years to come.

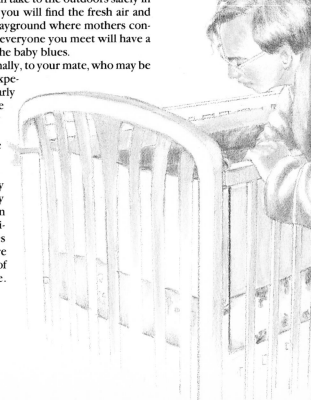

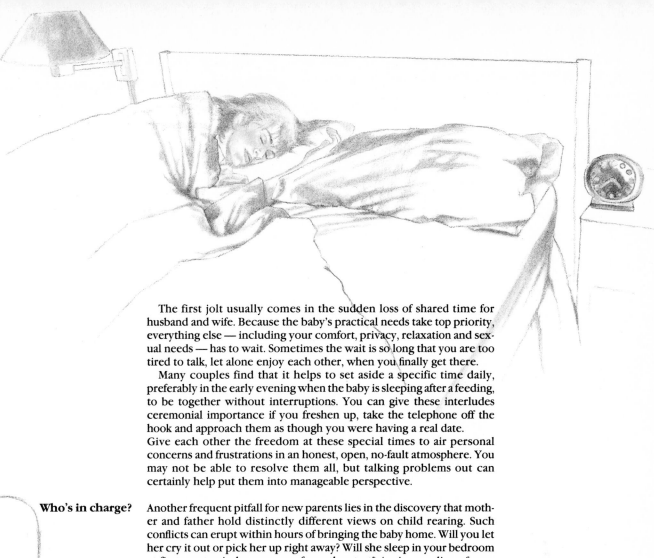

The first jolt usually comes in the sudden loss of shared time for husband and wife. Because the baby's practical needs take top priority, everything else — including your comfort, privacy, relaxation and sexual needs — has to wait. Sometimes the wait is so long that you are too tired to talk, let alone enjoy each other, when you finally get there.

Many couples find that it helps to set aside a specific time daily, preferably in the early evening when the baby is sleeping after a feeding, to be together without interruptions. You can give these interludes ceremonial importance if you freshen up, take the telephone off the hook and approach them as though you were having a real date.

Give each other the freedom at these special times to air personal concerns and frustrations in an honest, open, no-fault atmosphere. You may not be able to resolve them all, but talking problems out can certainly help put them into manageable perspective.

Who's in charge? Another frequent pitfall for new parents lies in the discovery that mother and father hold distinctly different views on child rearing. Such conflicts can erupt within hours of bringing the baby home. Will you let her cry it out or pick her up right away? Will she sleep in your bedroom at first or stay in her nursery from the start? Again, a policy of easy communication between parents, coupled with some flexibiity and willingness to compromise, will enable most couples to resolve these differences fairly smoothly.

Division of labor The issue of parental roles is yet another bone of contention in some households: How much responsibility for practical care should fall to the mother and how much to the father? Many a new mother comes home expecting the father to share equally in the routines of parenting, only to discover that the mate who kept faithfully by her side during labor and delivery now shows little interest in changing even an occasional diaper or giving a late-night bottle.

Despite notable attitude changes in recent years, society still largely predisposes females to be the primary caregivers and males to feel somewhat uncomfortable handling babies on a day-to-day basis. It is not unusual for a new father to see his wife as having the inside track with the baby and himself as something of an outsider. He may turn his energies to being the traditional good provider and withdraw both physically and emotionally, driven by a self-imposed pressure to work harder at his job. Ironically, this withdrawal often takes place just when his mate needs him most for practical help and emotional support.

Sexual feelings   Perhaps the most difficult issue for new parents to deal with is the resumption of normal sexual intimacy. Physically, intercourse is safe as soon as the woman's cervix has returned to normal and her episiotomy or cesarean incision, if any, has healed — generally about six weeks after delivery. But even when physical recovery is complete, many new mothers wait months for their sexual responsiveness to return to normal. The reasons for this are complex and may range from simple fatigue or self-consciousness over her still-flabby body to a temporary redirection of her affections to the new baby. And it is not uncommon for an already-shaky session of love-making to come to an untimely end when it is interrupted by a burst of fussing from the baby.

A nursing mother is particularly prone to difficulties. Often her breasts become extremely tender as a result of their distention, or they may temporarily lose all sensation. Sexual orgasm can add to the discomfort when it triggers a hormonal response that causes breast milk to leak copiously. Hormones related to lactation also reduce vaginal lubrication, which can make intercourse painful.

Facing all these obstacles, a new father may well fear that he has been displaced by the newborn, that his mate no longer cares for him, that in the enthusiasm of his love-making he may hurt her or that passion has permanently abandoned their marriage.

Such conflicts are natural and should be kept in perspective during these early weeks; allowing sexual pressures to build will only aggravate a situation that is already strained. You should approach the issue of sex as sensibly as you would any other practical problem. Find ways to give each other physical pleasure without intercourse until your obstetrician has lifted the ban on sex. When you are ready to resume full relations, have the doctor recommend lubricating preparations and physical positions that will ease any initial discomfort. You will find that time and patience are natural solutions for sexual readjustment as well as for a host of other problems that may present themselves during the early days of parent-

Survival Strategies for the Early Weeks

Set priorities: Decide what is most important, do that first and try not to fret about the rest. Write down a hierarchy of your family's physical, emotional and practical needs — from shared time, rest and nutritious meals to clean laundry and phone calls. As each new demand appears, put it to the test: How important is it compared to the major priorities in your life?

Be organized: Keep a running list of big and small tasks as the first step in getting them under control. Set aside specific times to make phone calls, pay bills or write baby announcements. Break large projects into small segments and do the most important parts first. Pack for outings well in advance, to avoid any last-minute confusion.

Take all the help you can get: Buy individual laundry baskets and ask family members to put away their own clothes. Suggest that friends bring in a ready-to-serve evening meal in lieu of a baby gift. Let neighbors run local errands for you. Hire a cleaning service or housekeeper for a weekly heavy cleaning. Get a high-school student to help with minor chores.

Simplify household routines: Set a timer for 15 minutes and stick to a simple straightening-up routine — washing dishes, making beds, clearing clutter — or whatever gives you the greatest sense of order with the least effort. Cook meals in large batches and freeze portions for later. Consolidate baby equipment on lazy Susans in the kitchen and nursery.

Go for convenience: Pretend you are on vacation and take labor-saving shortcuts whenever possible for the first month. Use paper plates and plastic forks; send shirts out to be laundered and ironed; have pizza or Chinese food delivered to your home. Buy disposable diapers and premixed bottles of formula for now. Think of it as spending money in order to save your own energy — your most precious resource of all, at this stage.

Make time to relax: Do any cooking and cleaning in the morning, to have it out of the way. As you work, listen to soothing music on the radio or stereo. Rest when the baby rests; the piled-up chores will wait. Take your phone off the hook during naptime. Or get an answering machine and tape a cheery message giving your baby's vital statistics and saying that you will be recuperating for a few days. Hang a note by your doorbell explaining the same. At least once a day, take a break from the house and go strolling outdoors with the baby, who might be feeling as bored and restless as you are.

hood. Patience, in fact, may turn out to be the most important parental skill you ever develop. Whether you welcome them or not, the baby will impose a whole new set of priorities on your family life. Schedules are bound to be disrupted while you and your family adjust to the new baby, and you will need to make allowances for inevitable delays in getting to an appointment, preparing a meal or simply getting the laundry done. Many days you will probably find your list of things to do has grown longer rather than shorter by the end of the day. You will need to develop an aggressive new approach to time management.

At the beginning, you should forget about well-kept schedules and housekeeping standards and focus on simple survival. Keep reminding yourself that nothing is more important to you and the baby right now than rest, recuperation from the physical effects of childbirth and relaxing in each other's company.

As your little one grows, your priorities will constantly shift to keep pace with his development and his changing needs — and with your own growing competence at the complex job of parenting. Looking back, you will probably be surprised at how swiftly the beleaguered newborn phase evolved into a life that is quite sane and manageable. Still, in many ways — most of them wonderful — your grown-up existence will never be the same. •⁙•

Everyday Care

As any new parent can tell you, the basic physical care of an infant involves a formidable amount of busywork. In the early weeks especially, life seems like a merry-go-round of repetitive acts: changing diapers, giving sponge baths, tugging tiny undershirts on and off, folding and unfolding the stroller, rocking the inexplicably fussy baby to sleep — or waiting for him to wake up so it can begin all over again. No wonder so many new mothers reach afternoon's end weary and frustrated, feeling that a whole day has passed with nothing to show for it and worrying, perhaps, that there is not enough quality time to relax and play and get to know the little person at the hub of all this activity.

Certainly, you can streamline your daily routines by having the right equipment on hand and by mastering the practical baby-care techniques described in the pages that follow. But you can also take comfort from the fact that you are accomplishing a great deal during those seemingly insignificant moments in your baby's first year. At no other time in your child's life are you as physically close to him as when you are performing the mundane rituals of changing and bathing and dressing. And what better time for spontaneous play, for the face-to-face chatting and tummy-tickling games that can turn a perfunctory chore into a moment of shared fun?

Moreover, each time you pick up and soothe your infant when he cries or relieve the discomfort of his clammy diaper, he learns to trust you a little more, to depend on you as someone who can be counted on to make things right. And you, in turn, come to understand your baby and his needs even better as you observe the shifting patterns of his sleeping and waking, his fussing and smiling — all part of the dramatic pageant of development that unfolds during the first 12 months.

By year's end, you will discover that you and your baby know and love each other very well — which is about as much quality as you can ask of any time.

Outfitting the Nursery

There is so much useful-looking equipment in a baby-products store that you may feel the impulse to buy all your nursery furnishings immediately. It is wiser to consider first how the baby's things are going to fit into your home and to weigh the possibilities of borrowing equipment or adapting furniture that you already have. Most baby equipment is, after all, usable only for a few months.

Planning the nursery

Whether you have a separate room for your infant or will be squeezing the nursery into a small apartment, you will want a safe, quiet, convenient place for the baby. If your home has more than one level, you may want to have sleeping and changing accommodations both upstairs and down. Once you have decided where the baby will be, figure out space for these three essentials: a crib; a changing table; and shelves, drawers or baskets for storage. The crib is the largest piece of equipment, so you will usually arrange the other furniture around it. The changing table can be as simple as a wide, padded bureau, but it should incorporate some storage space for fresh baby clothes and diapers (*box, page 39*).

When you examine the equipment you are thinking about buying, make sure that it is solidly constructed and that there are no sharp edges on the hardware, no splinters in the wood, no tears in the vinyl or exposed X joints that could pinch or cut. And remember, neither high prices nor physicians' endorsements are a guarantee of quality.

The baby's first bed

A tiny newborn often looks lost in a crib, and some infants do in fact prefer a more confined space for their first three months. For this reason, many parents make the investment in a short-term bed such as a bassinet or cradle, which sometimes then becomes a treasured heirloom. But even a lined laundry basket will do nicely. Such small beds are portable enough to be set within arm's reach — a boon to tired parents in the middle of the night.

The crib is the acquisition that requires the most careful attention, particularly from the standpoint of safety (*box, right*). In addition to the crib itself, you will need a mattress, a waterproof sheet, a quilted crib pad, fitted sheets, blankets and bumper pads to ring the edges of the mattress. Babies do not, however, need pillows and can actually smother on them, so keep them out of the crib. You may also discover the need for a portable crib. Among the styles available are folding mesh-walled models, which make convenient beds away from home, and minicribs, which you can roll easily from room to room.

Optional equipment

Your baby's and your own preferences can be your guide in deciding whether to invest in such nursery extras as playpens, infant seats, doorway jumpers, walkers and swings. These items are helpful in that they free up your hands for other chores, so you are likely to want at least one of them. But be aware that such furnishings are not baby-sitters — they should be used sparingly and always with supervision. Read the manufacturer's instructions for safety considerations.

Features of a Safe Crib

teething guard

snug-fitting mattress

bumper pad

high rail

secure
drop-side latches

closely spaced slats

simple end panel

Mattress. *Fit is essential: If you can get more than two fingers between the mattress and crib wall, you have a gap that can trap a baby's head. The mattress should be firm to support the infant's developing body.*

Bumper pads. *These protective pads should fasten snugly to the crib slats in at least six places. If your bumper pads have ties, cut off the loose ends so that the baby does not chew on them. Remove the pads*

when your infant can pull herself upright, or the child may use them to climb out of the crib.

Teething guards. *Make sure that these plastic bars capping the top crib rails are firmly attached and in good condition. Any guard that is beginning to crack should be removed promptly.*

Drop-side latches. *The mechanisms that fasten the lowering sides of the crib should be babyproof. The safest latches require two separate actions in order to release: One type has a foot-operated latch that you can release only while pulling upward on the railings.*

End panels. *Plain, functional headboards and footboards are safer than those with ornate cutouts or built-in toys. Endboards that extend down to the floor will discourage crawlers from playing under the crib. If a crib has corner posts, they should rise no more than five*

eighths of an inch above the rails, to prevent clothing from catching on them.

Slats. *Measure to be sure that the slats are spaced no more than two and three eighths inches apart. Do not use an old crib that has missing slats.*

Rails. *To discourage climbing, the crib rails should be a minimum of 22 inches above the mattress in its lowest position.*

Paints and finishes. *The surfaces of the crib should be smooth and free of flaking. When you refinish a crib, use high-quality nontoxic enamel paint. Check the label for warnings against use on baby furniture.*

Crib toys. *Mobiles that hang on the crib should be taken down by about three months, before the child is able to break off small pieces. Remove larger toys when the child is old enough to stand on them.*

The playpen, now sometimes called a play yard, provides a comfortable area in which a baby can enjoy his toys. It can be used until the baby is about 18 months to two years old and then will double as a storage bin. The traditional slatted playpen, although cagelike, helps the child develop grasping and pulling-up skills. Softer mesh-walled playpens prevent head injuries if a baby falls against the sides.

Infant seats, which are usable for the baby's first six months or so, let you take your child anywhere in the house and prop him up for a look at the world. Some parents also use infant seats for feedings while their babies are too small for high chairs. Look for a model with a base that is wider than the seat and with nonskid bottom surfaces.

Automatic swings provide a soothing motion that keeps many infants quite content. Some parents have found them effective in pacifying tense or colicky babies. Before you buy, however, be sure that the wide-spreading legs of a swing do not pose a space problem in your home.

Doorway jumpers are also great fun for most babies because they allow them to exercise by bouncing off the tips of their toes. Jumpers can be used from the time a baby can hold his head and neck up well — about four months — until he is steadier on his feet and beginning to cruise. Before you buy a jumping toy, make sure that the moldings around your door are solid enough to support the baby's weight.

Walkers, tiny seats on wheels, let babies move around before they can walk. While the walker is one of the most popular pieces of baby equipment, it is also one of the most potentially dangerous ones, easy for an active baby to propel at high speeds or tip over. Therefore, you should always watch your child closely when he is playing in a walker. ∴

Holding and Handling Your Baby

Babies love to be held. Whether you cuddle, cradle or rock them, infants are comforted and soothed by this earliest and most basic form of communication. Some experts believe, in fact, that babies who receive regular, close contact in infancy grow into more affectionate and responsive children.

While most parents are intuitively drawn toward physical contact with a newborn child, they are not innately skilled in holding or handling a baby smoothly and safely. Awkward handling may cause your child to cry or become fidgety — which makes him all the more difficult to calm and control. In the natural course of getting adjusted to your child, you would soon develop a comfortable and comforting way to hold him that would suit both of you just fine, without any advice from anybody. But the tips illustrated on these pages can speed that development by giving you the assurance that you are handling your baby safely.

Since newborns are startled by loud noises and sudden movements, always approach your infant calmly and alert him to your presence by talking to him or letting him see you before you begin to move him. Although newborns are not as fragile as they seem, you should always lift and lower your baby in smooth,

flowing motions, holding him firmly and making sure to support his head and neck. In both instances, bend over him and keep him close to your body, so he will not suffer the sensation of moving unsupported through space.

For a very young baby, suit the hold to what you are doing, using both hands for cuddling or communicating, but freeing up a hand for other purposes by letting the child ride in the so-called football carry on your forearm. You should also adapt the hold to the baby's age and level of muscle control. By three months, your child may wriggle so much that you have to replace single-arm holds with two-handed grips. And even though his head control improves markedly after three months, you should continue to use holds that provide head and neck support for several more months. By six months, your baby needs less careful handling and can generally support his neck and head by himself. He will start to balance himself as he rides on your hip, holding on with his legs and shifting his weight when you bend. Remember, however, that your child's increasing weight places added strains on your own muscles. Avoid the hip hold in particular if you suffer from weak or injured lower-back muscles.

Picking Up and Laying Down

Face-up lifting. *To lift a baby lying on his back, slide one hand under his neck to support his head and the other hand under his bottom. Bend over, gently draw the baby to your chest and slowly stand up. To put the baby down, reverse the procedure, letting his head and shoulders touch down just before his bottom.*

Face-down lifting. *To lift a baby lying on his stomach, slide one arm under his shoulder and neck, supporting his head as shown above. Slide the other arm between his legs, using that hand to support his trunk and thighs. Then gently raise him off the mattress. Use the same hold to lower a baby onto his stomach.*

Holding Babies under Six Months

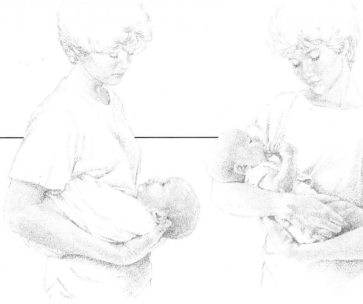
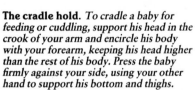

The football hold. *To carry an infant while keeping one hand free, slide your forearm under his back, supporting his neck and head with your hand as shown above. Press his trunk gently but firmly against your side with his head facing you and his feet tucked under your elbow.*

The cradle hold. *To cradle a baby for feeding or cuddling, support his head in the crook of your arm and encircle his body with your forearm, keeping his head higher than the rest of his body. Press the baby firmly against your side, using your other hand to support his bottom and thighs.*

The shoulder hold. *For maximum body contact, draw the baby toward your chest with one forearm bracing his back and your hand cradling his head. Support your baby's bottom and thighs with your other forearm and gently press his head against your shoulder.*

Three Holds for Older Babies

A face-down hold. *For two-handed carrying, place the baby face down with one forearm supporting his chest. Slide your other arm between his legs so that your hand supports his trunk.*

A face-forward hold. *To share a view or event, draw your baby's back snugly against your chest with one hand propping up his bottom and the other hand or forearm pressed firmly against his chest.*

The hip hold. *To carry an older baby while keeping one hand free, draw him to your side with his legs straddling your hip. Support his back with your forearm and grip his torso with your hand.*

Diapers and Diapering

Changing diapers is nobody's favorite task, but it is a simple and straight-forward one that quickly becomes second nature. Newborns generally have to be changed 10 or more times a day: At that rate, a week will make you an expert. Cleaning the stools of an infant is not nearly so distasteful as many anticipate. But whether or not you adjust easily to the task, it is important not to make your baby feel that there is anything dirty or disgusting about his bowel or bladder functions. Many parents find diapering a good occasion for face-to-face chats or games. Prolonging time on the changing table also gives your baby's bottom a chance to air. If the child is a boy, however, keep a cloth over his penis or you may get squirted. As the baby gets older and squirmier, you will need distracting songs or toys to keep him peaceful for any length of time.

When to change

How often you should change diapers depends in part on how sensitive your baby's skin is. The drier you keep his bottom the better, but infants urinate so frequently that it is usually pointless to change diapers the minute they get damp. On the other hand, it is important to clean the child promptly after every bowel movement, because bacteria in babies' stools react with urine to create ammonia, a powerful irritant and one of the causes of diaper rash. Diapers that are merely wet can usually be changed at routine intervals — after each nap, before each feeding. If diaper rash sets in, however, more frequent changes may be needed.

Monitoring a baby's bowels

The frequency, color and consistency of a baby's stools can vary considerably in the first weeks of life. The sticky, black meconium left over from the womb will probably all be passed in the first few days. This may be followed by frequent, loose, greenish stools as the child's system adjusts to the novelty of food. After a few weeks, most babies settle into a regular pattern of bowel movements, though there may still be variation. Anything from several movements a day to one every several days is regarded as normal. The stools of a breast-fed baby are usually a yellowish paste with a mildly sour odor. Stools of bottle-fed babies are generally browner and firmer, with a smell more like that of adult stools.

Routine fluctuations in frequency and color are usually nothing to worry about. Significant changes in consistency and frequency, however, may be signs of a problem. Breast-fed babies are almost never constipated and are rarely subject to diarrhea. Bottle-fed babies are more prone to such digestive difficulties, and their stools are an early indicator. Babies often strain, grunt and gurgle when moving their bowels, but

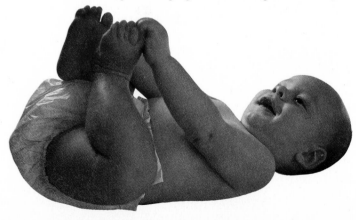

A Changing Table Designed for Convenience

The key to trouble-free diaper changing is preparation — having your supplies ready at hand. The place to gather everything is the changing table. In a large house, you may even want to set up two changing stations to save steps during the early months of frequent changes. Well-designed changing tables are readily available at baby-products stores, but a homemade one will work just as well. All that is needed is a large, padded surface with plenty of storage space underneath. An old dresser will do nicely, but it should be about waist high or you will tire your back with the constant bending over. A baby-carriage mattress makes a good pad for a makeshift changing table. The table should also have hanging trays or a wall-mounted shelf, on which to assemble your baby-cleaning supplies, and a belt with which to restrain the child. But no matter how secure-ly the baby is strapped, never leave him unat-tended on the table. Everything you need should be within arm's reach so that you can al-ways keep one hand on your child.

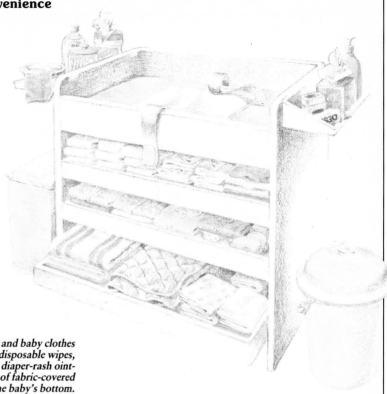

This changing table provides easy access to diapers and baby clothes as well as diaper-changing essentials: tissues, disposable wipes, cotton balls, cotton-tip swabs, baby oil and lotion, diaper-rash oint-ment, a small bowl for warm water, and squares of fabric-covered rubber sheeting to place under the baby's bottom.

this is nothing to be alarmed about unless the stool is hard and passed with obvious discomfort. You should check a baby's diaper after every feeding, since the gastrointestinal reflex prompts the elimination of feces whenever food is taken in. This can be inconvenient if the child has drifted off to sleep, but reducing the chance of diaper rash by changing the diaper is worth the risk of waking the baby up.

Cloth versus disposable diapers
By the time your baby is a few days old, you will want to decide whether to use cloth diapers or disposables. Essentially, it is a choice between economy and convenience. Over the two and a half years you are likely to use them, cloth diapers — also available in prefolded form — work out to be significantly cheaper than disposables, even including the initial cost of three or four dozen diapers, a dozen or so plastic pants and all the detergent, sterilizer, electricity and gas you will use to clean them. On the other hand, using disposables saves you the trouble of soaking, washing, rinsing, drying and folding cloth diapers. A third alter-native, a diaper service, guarantees sterile diapers free of chemical residues. This arrangement is just about as convenient as disposables, but also just about as expensive — unless you have more than one child in diapers, in which case a service is quite a bit cheaper.

In recent years, a large majority of American parents have opted for disposable diapers. In addition to being maintenance-free, they are easi-er to put on, requiring no folding, no plastic pants and no pins, which make some parents nervous. Unlike home-washed diapers, disposables carry no residues of either bacteria or washing chemicals, both of which can contribute to diaper rash. They are particularly handy when you are away from home. On the other hand, maintaining your supply requires frequent trips to the store, and disposables are expensive. And you may have to try several brands before you find one that meets your needs for durability and absorbency.

Some manufacturers claim their disposables — or at least the paper lining — can be flushed down the toilet. This practice invites plumbing problems. It is safer and easier to throw used disposables in a lidded diaper pail lined with a plastic trash bag. For soiled ones, first shake or scrape as much of the stool as you can into the toilet, then wrap the diaper into a tight bundle — with the soiled surface inside — and fasten it together with one of the sticky tabs before discarding it in the pail.

Washing cloth diapers

Cleaning cloth diapers is a multistep process. As with disposables, soiled cloth diapers must be shaken or scraped off. But they must also be rinsed, either in the toilet or the sink, and then soaked in a disinfectant solution in a diaper pail, along with the diapers that were merely wet. There are several disinfectants manufactured for this purpose, but you can also use simple borax. The pail should be the largest size that you can conveniently carry when filled from the changing area to the washing machine. Soak the dirty diapers for about six hours, then wash them with a low-sudsing detergent and the hottest possible water. Some doctors recommend a mild soap rather than detergent. Either way, the important thing is to rinse out all the chemicals after the wash. This takes at least two hot rinses, possibly three. Do not use fabric softeners in the washer or antistatic paper squares in the dryer; both contain irritating chemicals. Finally, fold the diapers to ready them for use.

Dealing with diaper rash

Diaper rash usually starts as a simple sore bottom, a red area of irritation caused by a strongly alkaline or strongly acidic bowel movement, or by just a soiled or wet diaper left on too long. At this point, all that is needed is rinsing the area with water and then drying it thoroughly, perhaps with a hair dryer set on low temperature. Follow up with more frequent changes and leave off the plastic pants to allow more air to reach the baby's bottom. Some parents apply petroleum jelly or zinc oxide ointment to prevent further irritation. If the condition persists or gets worse, try keeping the diapers off altogether for as long as you conveniently can; outdoors in the sunshine is best, though you have to be careful of sunburn. If you wash your own diapers, be particularly careful about rinsing them thoroughly and add a half cup of white vinegar to the last rinse to help fight bacteria.

Sometimes a simple diaper rash is complicated by a bacterial or yeast infection. A bacterial infection may cause fluid-filled blisters or pimples. A yeast infection produces a bumpy rash of fiery red spots. In either case, a doctor should be consulted. The skin of some babies is irritated by ingredients in disposable wipes and lotions; in such cases, the problem clears up when use of the products is discontinued. ❖

Diaper-Changing Techniques

Cleaning Up after a Messy Diaper

Cleaning the baby's bottom. *Use the unsoiled front of the old diaper to wipe away most of the stool, then follow up with tissues, toilet paper or disposable wipes to remove any traces of stool that remain. Lay a towel under the baby's bottom and gently wash the soiled area with a washcloth or cotton balls dipped in warm water. When you remove a particularly messy diaper, you may find it more practical simply to wash the baby's bottom in the bathroom sink, after an initial wipe-off. Dry the baby thoroughly with a towel.*

Cleaning a boy's genitals. *Wash the genitals of both circumcised and uncircumcised boys with plain warm water and a washcloth or cotton balls. Do not pull back the foreskin of an uncircumcised child to wash underneath. While a circumcised child is still healing, wipe the penis gently, then coat it with petroleum jelly and cover it with a gauze square before diapering.*
Cleaning a girl's genitals. *Clean with downward strokes, from her front to her back, using a clean cotton ball for each wipe. Do not wipe away any whitish vaginal discharge; these are natural secretions that protect the delicate tissues.*

Putting on a Clean Diaper

Prefolded cloth diapers. *Before putting the diaper on the baby, fold the longer edges toward the center at one end to form a wedge. Slide the diaper under the baby, with the narrow end of the wedge in front and the back edge aligned with his waist. Fold up the front, then bring the back corners around on top of it. Keeping your fingers between the cloth and the baby, pin the corners. Use sharp pins; coating the points with soap or petroleum jelly will make it easier to push them through cloth. If the baby's umbilical cord has not healed, fold down the front of the diaper to keep the cord exposed to the air.*

Disposables. *The tapes on a disposable diaper are on the back side. Slide that side under the baby's bottom with the top edge roughly at the child's waist. Fold the front up against the baby's stomach and pull the tapes around to attach in front, being careful not to bind the child too tightly. If a tape tears or fails to stick, fasten the diaper with masking tape. On a newborn, fold the front of the diaper down away from the umbilical cord until the stump has healed.*

Bathtime

Babies react in different ways to the experience of bathing. The majority find it a real delight and show their enjoyment with nonstop swishing and splashing, but others balk at the sensation right from the start. Parents are more predictable. Most are nervous at first, unsettled by the idea of holding a slippery infant in a tub of soapy water, but with a little practice even the most anxious quickly become relaxed.

When should the baby be bathed?

A babe in arms does not have to be bathed every day. Until she is able to crawl on the floor, she does not have much chance to get dirty. Therefore, as long as you clean her carefully when you change diapers and after feedings, two or three baths a week should suffice. When the youngster starts to crawl or starts to feed herself, however, a daily bath will probably become a necessity.

Bathtime can be any time of day, but it should jibe with your baby's sleep schedule. Some mothers find that their babies are most receptive before the midmorning feeding; other mothers prefer an early-evening bath because it leaves the child relaxed for bed.

The bathroom and the kitchen are the most common places for bathing babies, but as long as the infant is small enough to bathe in a portable tub, you can use any room in the house. The temperature of the room is an important factor, however: It should be at least 75° F. and free of drafts. The water in the bath should be close to the infant's skin temperature, around 90° F., and should feel pleasantly warm to you. Use your elbow or the inside of your wrist to test the water; your hands are not sensitive enough to judge water temperature well.

Cleaning a newborn's scalp

Washing a newborn's scalp, with its soft spots and susceptibility to the condition called cradle cap, makes many parents understandably uneasy. Actually, the temporary gaps in the bones of the skull, called fontanels, are covered by a tough protective membrane. They do require gentleness, but there is no need to avoid touching them. Cradle cap *(page 17)* is a waxy, dandruff-like crust that forms in patches on the scalp of many young babies; it is harmless but unattractive. To help prevent it, shampoo the infant's hair each time you bathe her.

If your infant does get cradle cap, try massaging the scalp with a soft

baby brush as you shampoo, or rub the scalp with baby oil before you shampoo to loosen the crust.

Nose and ears In your effort to keep your baby beautiful, you may be tempted to scrub wax out of her ears and mucus out of her nose. But even gently handled, cotton swabs will most likely succeed only in packing the wax into the ear. Moreover, earwax is naturally antiseptic; if you remove it, the ears will only produce more. The delicate membranes in the nose are easily scratched, even with sterile cotton. When you clean the nose and ears, therefore, it is best simply to wipe around the outside as best you can.

Body creases and genitals Be thorough in cleaning and drying the baby's body creases, where moisture tends to become trapped and irritate the skin. Run a soapy finger along all the creases: on the neck, behind the knees and elbows, between the buttocks and elsewhere. Then rinse well and dry carefully.

There is no need to clean inside a girl's genitals; simply wash the exterior, working from the front toward the anus. An uncircumcised boy's penis does not require special care, either; because the foreskin does not naturally retract until the age of four years or later, parents should not attempt to clean under it. Simply wipe the exterior of your son's penis and scrotum clean, whether he is circumcised or not.

Powdering a baby after a bath is unnecessary, and in fact many doctors recommend against it, since the powder tends to cake and cause irritation. If you do use powder, apply it with the palm of your hand rather than sprinkling it directly from the can, to prevent the baby from inhaling the fine dust. And be sure the powder you choose does not contain talc, which can be harmful to the baby's lungs.

Right after a bath is the best time to trim a baby's nails, while they are still soft and pliable. Use small, blunt-tipped scissors and cut straight across the nails, taking care not to leave any jagged corners. If your baby resists, perform the process while she sleeps. Begin nail-trimming at three or four weeks, or sooner if the baby's nails are long.

Bathtime fears If a baby under six months old protests when you bathe her, she is probably sensitive to the temperature of the room or the water, or perhaps she feels unstable propped up in the tub. If necessary, go back to sponge-bathing *(page 44)* for a few weeks to give her time to outgrow her anxieties. Emphasize the play possibilities of bathing by letting her dabble her fingers in a bowl of water or her tub.

An older baby may begin to have genuine fears of the bath, but these are generally short-lived and rooted in experiences like getting water or soap in the eyes or slipping in the tub. Some babies simply fear the large size of the grown-up bathtub; in this case, try using the familiar portable tub inside the regular tub for a while, or get in the bath with your baby until she becomes accustomed to the big tub.

Getting their hair washed is the real bugaboo for most babies. The root of the problem is that children simply do not like water in their eyes. To keep a baby's face dry while shampooing, you can wet and rinse her hair with a washcloth, rather than pouring the water over her hair. Or you may wish to try using a halo-shaped headband designed for this purpose. Sometimes by eliminating this single problem of hair-washing, you can transform routinely unhappy baths into one of the highlights of each day. ⁘

Tailoring the Bath to the Baby

A Sponge Bath for the Newborn

During a sponge bath, keep your baby clothed except for the part of her body you are working on. This is ideal for a newborn, since it protects against chills and also keeps the navel dry while it is healing. Sponge baths are also good for quick cleanups on an older baby and for times when your child is too ill for bathing in the tub.

To give a sponge bath, you will need to arrange a towel-covered surface within reach of a sink or bowl of warm water and have ready a clean diaper and clothes. Also assemble beforehand cotton balls and swabs, a soft washcloth and towel, rubbing alcohol and baby shampoo. Plain water will do for newborns; their skin is too sensitive for soap. But a mild shampoo may help prevent cradle cap.

Pay special attention to the body creases and tiny spaces between the fingers and toes. While the umbilical stump is healing, keep it dry and clean it with rubbing alcohol; after it has dropped off, continue to dab the center of the navel with alcohol until it has stopped oozing.

Cleaning the face. *Clean each eye with a fresh cotton ball dipped in warm water, wiping out from the nose. Use more cotton to clean around the ears; wipe the mouth and chin with a washcloth.*

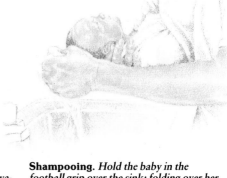

Shampooing. *Hold the baby in the football grip over the sink; folding over her earlobes with your hand will block the ear canals. Wet her scalp; shampoo with a soft cloth or your hand, rinse and dry.*

Washing the upper body. *Remove the baby's shirt and wipe her neck, chest, arms and hands; pat dry. Turn the baby on her side to wash her back, then dry her and put a clean shirt on her.*

Cleaning the lower body. *Remove the diaper and wash the baby's bottom and genitals. Wipe her legs, feet and between her toes. Dry your baby well before putting a fresh diaper on her.*

Cleaning the umbilical cord. *Fold down the front of the diaper and rub the stump of the umbilical cord with a cotton ball soaked in rubbing alcohol. Leave the diaper folded under the cord.*

Graduating to a Tub Bath

When the navel has stopped oozing, it is time to introduce your baby to bathing in a tub — usually a small, portable plastic tub to start. Fill the tub only a few inches deep and always test the water before putting the baby in. Do not try to add hot water once the child is in the tub; this could easily scald your baby.

The tubs come in a range of styles. Many parents buy special plastic tubs that are designed to hold the child at a convenient angle just beside or inside the kitchen sink. Some models come with foam pads, but these tend to become breeding grounds for bacteria and should be avoided. Plastic dishpans or the kitchen sink itself will also work, as long as you lay a towel on the bottom to prevent slipping. If you use the sink, swing the faucet away from the baby. Placing the tub at waist level will make bathtime easier on your back.

The bath itself changes little. Continue to wash the baby's face with plain water and to shampoo his hair as you did when he was younger, but now you can use a mild, unscented soap on the rest of his body. Rinse completely, however; soapy residue will dry and irritate his skin.

After about six months, your baby will have to begin bathing in the regular tub. But even after the child can sit up steadily by himself, you must never leave him alone, even for a moment. The possibility of the baby slipping and drowning in just a few inches of water is far too great to take any chances. Take the phone off the hook during bathtime or ignore the calls that you receive. If you must respond to an interruption, take the baby with you.

As a rule, keep one hand on the baby at all times and use your other hand for washing. A towel or bath mat under the child's bottom will cut down on sliding. There are also various kinds of bathtub seats and rings that keep an active child seated safely upright. Most of these de-vices attach to the tub bottom with suction cups; bear in mind that a bath mat or a rough surface may prevent the suction cups from adhering properly.

Toys will help focus the baby's attention on fun in the water and may cut down on squirming and attempts to stand up. But keep the soap out of the child's hands or it will surely end up in his eyes and mouth. If your baby tries to reach for the shiny faucets and handles, cover them with a towel so that he does not get burned on a hot faucet or bump his head on the plumbing fixtures.

Bathing a child in the big tub is an awkward exercise at best. If you kneel beside the tub, there will be less bending over and less strain on your back. Have all of your supplies laid out on the floor beside you. And when you lift the baby out, hold him under the armpits, keeping your back straight and letting your legs take as much of the strain as possible.

Lifting the baby. *To move her in or out of the tub, support her head and shoulders with your forearm and grasp her under one arm. Hold her thighs with your other hand, cradling her legs and bottom.*

A secure hold in the tub. *Support the baby in a partially upright position, using one hand and forearm. Use your other hand to wash and rinse the child's body.*

Sitting safely in the big tub. *Even after the baby can sit up unassisted, keep a hand on his arm — or at least close enough so that you can move quickly to assist him if he loses his balance.*

Your Baby's Wardrobe

Resist the temptation to buy a lavish layette months in advance of your child's birth. The stores will still be open after he is born, and you may welcome the excuse for shopping trips. Remember that baby showers, birth gifts and hand-me-downs may furnish many of your initial needs. And if your baby is typical, he will double his birth weight in five months, rapidly outgrowing all the clothes that fit him as a newborn.

A basic layette

Before the baby arrives, assemble a wardrobe of simple, inexpensive basics. The following items will meet most of the child's needs during the first six months.
- Cotton receiving blankets to wrap the infant in (three).
- Cotton undershirts, preferably the snap-up type that you do not have to pull over your baby's head (six).
- Grow bags or gowns with string-tied or snap-up bottoms that adjust easily as your baby grows (three).
- Stretch suits — one-piece coveralls for sleep or play (three).
- Sleeper — a heavier-weight coverall for winter wear (one).
- Snow suit, preferably two-piece with a hood for winter outings (one).
- Sweaters — finely woven to avoid tangling fingers (one to three).
- Hats — a broad-brimmed cotton hat for summer and a warm but lightweight machine-washable knitted cap that covers head and ears for winter (one of each).

Up to six months. *Convenience and adaptability are essential in younger infants' clothes: T-shirts that snap shut, drawstring gowns that open easily for diaper changes and stretch suits that can double as play suits or sleepers.*

Tips for buying infant apparel

Baby clothes should combine tough, durable construction with comfort and convenience. Look for sturdy necks and waistbands and for seams that are strong enough to withstand abuse, yet soft enough to prevent scratching. Buttons should be large enough to be manipulated by adult hands, and buttonholes should be bound with stitching. Look for extra lines of stitching where straps are joined to garments and for reinforcing tape around crotch snaps. Check that sleepwear meets federal requirements for flame resistance.

Most babies are comfortable in soft, absorbent fabrics that breathe — cottons and knits. Pass up frilly garments that require ironing. Pick clothes that facilitate diaper changes. As a practical consideration, buy items that are one or two sizes too large, or those that have growth features such as adjustable straps, grow tucks or undefined waists.

Dressing an older infant

By the sixth month, your child's increasing size and activity level call for clothes with different features and designs. To accommodate crawling and outdoor play, choose sturdy overalls and cotton T-shirts that slip over the baby's head. In summer, cotton shorts provide maximum coolness and freedom of movement. Dresses, although adorable, interfere with a crawling baby's mobility. Buy snow suits large enough to fit over indoor clothing; suits with separate tops and bottoms are more adaptable to temperature changes and can be easily removed for diaper changes. Hard-soled shoes are not recommended until your child begins to walk, because they may inhibit the growth of soft foot bones. Until then, use cloth booties or socks and sneakers. ∴

After six months. *For active older infants, garments such as snap-crotch overalls and two-piece snow suits provide protection and comfort while making diaper-changing easy.*

Taking the Dread Out of Dressing

For babies, dressing can be either a fun or alarming experience. And the methods you use to dress your infant — such as pulling a sleeve over the child's arm rather than tugging his arm through the sleeve — can make the difference. The dressing techniques that are illustrated and described below, combined with basic safety precautions and some light-hearted chatter or singing to distract the child, can turn this routine chore into a special time for both you and your baby.

Dress your baby in a comfortably warm room, between 70 and 75° F. In winter, you may want to warm sleepwear for a few minutes in the dryer or on a radiator, but make sure that snaps and zippers have cooled before you put the garment on the child. To avoid snagging your baby's skin, lift zippers away from the child's body before pulling them.

While babies love warmth, take care not to overdress your child; overheated babies may develop rashes and have trouble sleeping. Remember that your baby's comfort level is about the same as yours. But since an infant's hands and feet tend to be cold to the touch — because of his still-developing circulation — you should check for body temperature by touching the back of his neck. In winter and summer, you can follow the practice of experienced outdoorspeople, dressing your baby in layers that can be peeled off and put back on as the child moves between cooler and warmer spaces.

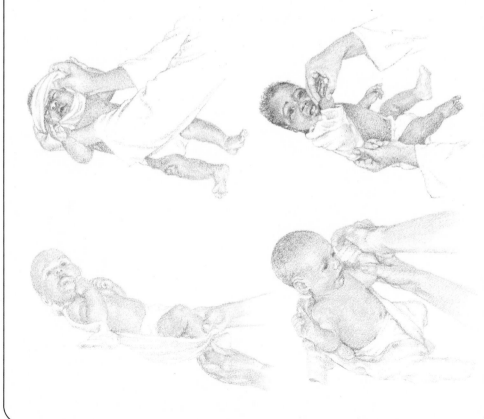

A pullover top. *First hand-stretch the neck and sleeve openings. Holding the neck opening in a loop (far left), slip the garment over your baby's head, stretching the opening so as not to block his nose and mouth or catch on his ears. Next, slip your hand into a sleeve opening from the outside and grasp your baby's hand (left). Then use your other hand to pull the sleeve over his arm. Repeat for the other arm.*

A one-piece suit. *To dress your baby in a one-piece suit or sleeper, lay the garment flat on a changing table or other secure surface. Place your baby face up on top of the suit. Lift each leg (far left) and slide his feet into the suit's legs. Then gather up each sleeve of the suit, place your baby's hand in the armhole and pull the sleeve over his arm. Snap or zip the suit shut.*

Crying and Comforting

New parents receive few guarantees, but one thing you can depend on is that your baby will cry. Doctors believe that an infant's crying in the early months is not only inevitable but necessary: It is the newborn's sole means of communicating her needs.

As a survival mechanism, a young infant's crying seems tuned for effectiveness: Studies have shown that the tone of a baby's cries can actually raise the heart rate and blood pressure of adults who hear the sound. Thus, along with their natural concern for the baby's comfort and safety, parents may feel a physiological need for relief from the child's crying that compels them to respond promptly with comfort, food or other assistance.

Most experts advise parents to respond immediately to their infant's cries, claiming that it is impossible to spoil a child under a year old with loving attention. In fact, studies have shown that when a parent responds quickly to a baby during the first six months, the child cries less later on in the first year. By meeting the needs of your young baby promptly and consistently, you increase the child's sense of control over her world, and in the process, help bolster her emotional security.

Swaddling to Soothe a Newborn

When bundled tightly in their blankets, babies often stop crying and drop off to sleep: It was this simple principle, no doubt, that led to the ancient custom of swaddling a newborn child. Although infants may appreciate any form of comforting confinement, especially one that provides warmth and restricts movement, the swaddling technique described below is usually quite successful. Swaddling works best with babies less than a month old; some experts believe it comforts babies by giving them a warm and secure feeling similar to that experienced in the womb. The close confinement also prevents the uncontrolled flailing of arms and legs that can agitate a baby. Once snugly wrapped, an infant may feel even more secure if she is wedged into a padded corner of the crib with her head and shoulder against the crib bumpers.

Place the baby on a blanket diagonally so that her head rests on one corner. Bring the right corner of the blanket across her left arm and, raising her right arm, tuck the blanket under her right side.

Lift the lower corner of the blanket, pull it upward across the baby's body and then secure the blanket under the infant's right side and shoulder.

Bring the left corner across the baby's body and tuck it under her left side. The corner under her head can be folded back, leaving the baby in a neat bundle.

Why young babies cry

A baby's earliest crying is a reflexive reaction to discomfiting changes in her body or the environment. To most parents, the cries all sound alike at first, but by the second month a mother or father can usually recognize the distinctive crying patterns that are caused by various sources of distress.

The most common causes of a young baby's crying are hunger, pain, loneliness, overstimulation, fatigue, or discomfort from being too hot, too cold or trapped in a wet or messy diaper. About one in five new babies also suffers the extended crying bouts of the condition known as colic *(page 51)*.

Hunger

The kind of cry most parents will probably learn to recognize first is a rhythmic complaint consisting of a series of cries broken by brief pauses. This is how the baby tells you she is hungry, and normally she can be soothed simply by feeding. If these cries are left unanswered, they may turn into a steady howl.

When the baby is hungry, comfort can be supplied only by milk, and experts agree that she should have it without regard to any schedule. But do not assume too quickly that the problem is hunger, since overfeeding can cause stomach cramps and lead to more fussing. The child may be thirsty and need water or juice.

Pain

A shriek of pain is usually unmistakable, but its cause can be difficult to locate. You should look first for an open diaper pin, then for scratchy fabrics or other possible irritants. Air bubbles swallowed while a child is eating or crying are often quite painful. To relieve this discomfort, try holding your baby across your lap and pressing her stomach against your knees.

In older infants, pain may be caused by teething *(page 94)*. You should be alert, too, for signs of some illness that may be causing the baby physical distress. If fever, diarrhea or other symptoms of illness are present, or if the baby continues crying in apparent pain, telephone the child's physician.

Overstimulation

An overtired baby often uses a nasal whine to shut out unwanted stimulation and to release tension built up during the day's activities. If the baby has trouble relaxing and getting to sleep, you should consider cutting back slightly on her play and other vigorous activities.

Overstimulated babies may be soothed by the rhythmic sounds of soft music, talking, singing or humming; some mothers and fathers use recordings of a human heartbeat or of their baby's own cries to quiet the

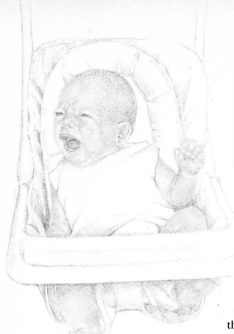

An infant swing. *The rhythmic motion of a portable baby swing can be comforting, especially for overstimulated babies. But don't leave your baby in a swing unless the movement calms him within 10 to 15 minutes.*

child. Even the steady drone of a fan or vacuum cleaner can be soothing.

Repetitive motions such as rocking and patting are also effective for overstimulated babies; researchers say that most children seem to respond best when rocking or swinging at the relatively fast rate of 60 rocks per minute, rather than at a slower pace. Sucking on a thumb, finger or pacifier is another repetitive motion that serves as a reliable tranquilizer for many children — and one that a resourceful baby can use to soothe herself while waiting for a caregiver to respond.

Loneliness

If your baby stops fussing when you pick her up, she may simply want to be held; she needs physical contact just as much as food and warmth. When you put her down and she starts crying again, this is her way of telling you she misses the secure feeling of being held in your arms. You might try taking the baby for a walk in a backpack or in a chest carrier, where she will be snug against your body and can listen to your heartbeat.

Crying in older babies

After the first six months, babies cry less frequently. Although continuing to communicate needs, tears now convey emotions as well — particularly fear and frustration. As babies try out new motor skills, they often cry when they are unable to go where they want or do what they want. The unfamiliar can also be frightening to older babies as they grow more independent and are able to explore. Having learned what is usual in her world, your child may become afraid when confronted with new people, places or experiences — in short, any break in her daily routine — and she may need an extra measure of reassurance from you at such times.

The importance of comforting

In addition to crying for these predictable and logical reasons, your child may at times fuss and cry for reasons you can neither determine nor influence, as changes in her fast-growing body and nervous system produce temporary disequilibrium or discomfort.

Nevertheless, the very act of attempting to comfort a crying baby is important to the child's well-being. Although it may not seem obvious at the moment, the bond between you and your child is strengthened each time she cries and you respond; even if she does not stop crying, she will be aware of the warmth and soft voice of the loving parent who is trying to make her feel better. •:•

The reliable pacifier. *Sucking contentedly on his pacifier, this baby blocks out disturbing stimuli and relaxes. Never put a pacifier on a ribbon around your baby's neck: he could become entangled in it.*

Understanding Colic

The word colic is widely misused. When babies cry for hard-to-determine reasons or are difficult to console, parents often describe them as colicky. But the term can properly be applied to only about 20 percent of all infants.

Colic, which I define as a period of extreme and unexplained fussiness, usually sets in during the third or fourth week after birth and lasts until the baby is three to four months old. Most babies pass in and out of fussy periods during the early months of life, and usually these last for only a few days; so you should not assume too quickly that your child's crying is caused by colic. Instead, use the following rule of thumb: If your baby cries inexplicably and is difficult to comfort for more than three hours a day at least three days a week, and if this pattern continues for three weeks, then colic is likely. Colic occurs among infants who are perfectly healthy in other ways; crying that is caused by illness or some other specific source of discomfort is unrelated to colic.

Because colic has never been well understood, a variety of myths have emerged to explain the condition — none of which, in my opinion, stand up to scientific scrutiny. Babies are equally prone to be colicky whether male or female, whether firstborn or preceded by older siblings and regardless of the educational or social status of the parents.

Perhaps the most harmful of the myths is the notion that colic is caused by anxiety in the mother. This is patently false; scientific research clearly points to physiological rather than environmental causes. For example, colic nearly always begins within two to three weeks after the expected date of birth, whether the baby is full-term or premature. If colic were caused by parental behavior, premature babies would develop colic much earlier than their full-term counterparts.

I also believe it a fallacy to think of colic as a gastrointestinal problem. The condition does not seem to be influenced by allergies, breast- or bottle-feeding, or what the baby or mother eats. Colicky babies show no sign of intestinal disorders. Stomach symptoms are usually a result rather than a cause of colic: During prolonged periods of crying infants swallow air, which is later expelled by burping or passing gas.

In my opinion, colic arises instead in the central nervous system — a reflection of normal changes in the brain as it matures during the early weeks of infancy. Notice your baby's random movements as he shudders, grimaces and twists in your arms. Within a few months, his brain will develop controls that inhibit or suppress these movements. All babies show this early lack of neurological control, but I believe colicky babies experience this unsettled phase earlier and more intensely. As a result, they are more wakeful, fussy and difficult to soothe.

The behavior associated with colic seems to parallel a new-born's sleep patterns. By the third or fourth month, a baby's brain has evolved a reliable day-and-night rhythm for waking and sleeping; it is probably no coincidence that the third or fourth month is also the time when colic disappears.

While time is the only real cure for colic, I believe that parents should respond quickly to the cries of a colicky baby and try to the best of their ability to soothe him. If comforting proves unsuccessful, and you feel that you need a break, putting the baby down to regain your strength will not harm your child. Some parents have had success with the so-called "colic hold" *(below)*. Cradling your baby comfortably in your arms, place one arm across his stomach and apply light pressure. Rock him gently, keeping his head slightly higher than his feet. Swaddling, rhythmic motion or sucking may also help.

Generally, I urge parents not to resort to medication or changing the baby's formula, but instead to continue trying comforting techniques — and reminding themselves that their child will soon outgrow the crying phase.

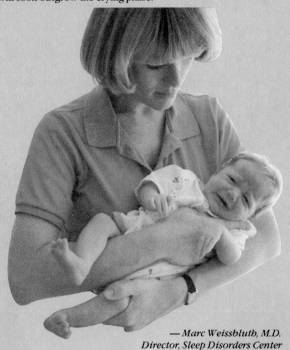

— Marc Weissbluth, M.D.
Director, Sleep Disorders Center
Children's Memorial Hospital, Chicago

Sleeping and Waking

In the newborn stage, each baby sleeps in a distinctive rhythm all his own. This cycle of sleeping and waking is apparently dictated by neurological signals and cannot be altered by anything a parent does. At this stage, your only influence on the process is to provide a comfortable bed and to counter disturbances that wake a child up. As the weeks go by and your baby becomes more responsive to the family environment, his sleeping patterns will gradually begin to conform to your own.

You may want the baby in your room at first, but within a few months you will probably prefer that he sleep in his own room where you can hear his cries without being disturbed by every movement. Keep his room relatively warm, 70° F. to 75° F. But there is no need to try to keep the house quiet; let him adjust to the normal level of household noise. An infant may be placed on his back or his stomach to sleep, but sleeping tummy-down restricts the random body movements that can disturb slumber and thus may help an infant sleep more soundly.

Sleep patterns   The sleep patterns of newborns vary greatly from infant to infant, but as babies grow older their sleep habits become more predictable. The average newborn sleeps or drowses for 16 to 20 hours a day, divided about equally between night and day. The baby's longest sleep period will generally be four or five hours, but some infants sleep only two hours at a time, while others may occasionally sleep as long as 10 hours. The sleep time gradually shifts toward night: At three months, babies average five hours of sleep during the day and 10 hours at night, usually with an interruption or two. At six months, they will nap about three hours during the day and sleep 11 hours at night. By the end of the first year the total sleep time decreases to about 13 hours.

Most babies will nap both mornings and afternoons for periods last-

ing anywhere from 20 minutes to four hours. If your baby sleeps a lot during the day, he may stay awake more at night. You may want to start his nap earlier in the afternoon and wake him after an hour or two.

Night waking

Babies generally begin sleeping through the night between four and six months of age, but at first this night may consist only of a stretch between midnight and five a.m. And even a baby who has begun sleeping through the night may go through spells of night waking. At these times, a quick response to the child's needs, whether for a drink or simply a comforting pat, will usually help him get right back to sleep. But there are other causes of night waking as well.

A baby's wakefulness sometimes reflects advances in his development. Learning a new skill such as pulling himself up in the crib excites a child and he may practice his new achievement at night. Some older babies wake up hungry at night, particularly when they are going through a growth spurt. And some six- to eight-month-olds work off energy by rocking on their hands and knees.

As your baby gains independence of movement, he may develop anxieties about separating from you, which can cause him to cry for you at night. Some babies form an attachment to a blanket or a particular toy animal; to some measure, such security objects can substitute for a parent's presence and help the child feel independent. If your child has a favorite object, give it to him as part of his bedtime routine.

When your baby wakes up in the morning, he may babble, watch his mobile or play independently in his crib for a while. There is no need to go to him the minute he wakes up; he will let you know by fussing or calling out when he needs your attention.

Early on, it is a good idea to settle your baby into a bedtime routine. He must learn to fall asleep by himself, and a good-night ritual is a reassuring send-off. This infant's routine includes a story on his mother's lap.

Sleep problems

If a baby wakes up five or six times in a night after six months of age, she has a problem, and you may need to consult her doctor. If her crying is uncharacteristic, you should check first for signs of illness. Once you have made sure that she is not sick, comfort and reassure her. Rather than picking her up, however, rub her back soothingly and leave her in bed. If you have to feed her, keep the socializing to a minimum. The next time she wakes up, try calling out to her to reassure her that you are there. Finally, give her 15 minutes to cry and she may settle down by herself. After you take this approach for several days, your baby should find it easier to get back to sleep on her own.

You and your child may have to work on her sleep schedule at various times during the first year and after. Try not to let it become a contest of wills. With patience and sensitivity to the particular needs of your baby, you can help her adjust to the sleep patterns of the rest of the family. •••

Getting Out and About

Most new mothers, after recovering from the physical effects of delivery, look forward to regaining their mobility as quickly as they can. Besides being a practical necessity, getting out and about is good for your health and mental well-being — and that, in turn, benefits your child. Basically, there are two things you will need to make outings possible: good, safe equipment in which to tote the infant when you bring him along and a trustworthy baby-sitter for the times when you leave your child behind.

Weather permitting, you can take a baby out as soon as you feel up to it yourself. However, for the first month, avoid exposing your infant to crowds or strangers, who may carry germs. To make excursions enjoyable for both you and the infant, anticipate his needs ahead of time. Whenever you leave the house, make sure you take along the necessary items to keep him fed, warm and dry *(box, right)*. You will also need to keep an eye open, wherever you go, for good places to change the baby and quiet spots for feedings.

The car seat   If you commonly travel by car, a car seat will be the most important piece of safety equipment you own — and probably the first one, as well. Most experts recommend buying one before the baby is born and bringing the infant home from the hospital in it. Car seats are now required by law in most states, but legalities aside, they are absolutely essential for keeping children safe in the car. A baby is simply not secure on your lap, no matter how firmly you hold him.

Numerous makes of car seats are well designed for the job, but for safety's sake, look for one that meets current federal motor vehicle safety standards. Look also for a seat that is easy to use. If you know you will frequently be moving the seat in and out of the car, find one that is compact enough to pass comfortably through the car doors. Consider also the ease of getting your baby in and out of the car seat: Some models have an elaborate system of buckles and straps, while others are very simple.

Try out the different car seats displayed in a baby-products store, and when you choose one, take the time to read carefully the instructions for installing and using it. Remember to adjust the harness straps periodically as your baby grows. Most important, strap the child in place every time you venture out in the car, even for short jaunts around town.

Baby carriers   Another consideration is your method of carrying the child once you are out of the car — or if your outing is simply a walk around the neigh-

A car seat is the only safe place for babies to sit in an automobile. The chair is anchored with the car's standard seat belts and often with special straps that bolt to the body of the car as well. Younger infants should ride in the back seat, facing the rear of the car.

The Complete Diaper Bag

What to look for:
- Durability. Check for strong seams and sturdy fasteners. Choose a dark color that will not show the dirt.
- Comfort. The bag should be easy to carry, with both a handle and an adjustable shoulder strap — ideally, one that will hang on your stroller.

What to bring:
- Disposable diapers.
- Waterproof squares for changing surfaces.
- Washcloth or disposable towelettes.
- A change of clothing.
- Diaper-rash ointment.
- Sunscreen.
- Bottles of water or formula and food. Bring unopened jars or dry foods that will not spoil.
- Plastic bags for soiled clothing.
- A pacifier.
- Small toys.

borhood. There are several options, depending on the baby's size. For newborns and infants up to about three or four months, a slinglike pack that holds the baby in front of you may be your choice, provided your back muscles can handle the weight. Infants like the security of being held close, and with the child's head just beneath your chin, you are well positioned to keep her contented. When using a carrier, be mindful of the baby's weak neck and support her head when you bend forward.

Front baby carriers become a strain on your shoulders and lower back, however, once the child weighs more than about 12 pounds. By switching to a backpack-style carrier, you can still keep your hands free while carrying a heavier child. The frame of a backpack distributes the baby's weight more evenly and will keep you more comfortable. With the baby out of view behind you, it is vital that you belt her into the carrier every time — especially when she reaches the stage of learning to stand.

The stroller   Some parents prefer a stroller for transporting a baby on minor shopping trips and walks around the block, and the ride is usually relaxing for the baby as well. When shopping for a stroller, look for one with a seat belt, a basket or pockets for carrying packages, washable upholstery and a sturdy frame that locks in place when the stroller is in use, so that it cannot collapse with the baby's bouncing. A good stroller should also be easy to fold up when not in use; before buying it, see if you can do so with one hand, as you would if you were rushing for a bus or taxi.

Long-distance travel   Making longer trips with a baby — extended drives or airplane flights, for instance — demands additional planning, but such journeys can be quite manageable if you are prepared. In fact, many parents find travel easier with an infant than with a toddler, who by the age of a year has developed more mobility and complex needs, as well as a distinct will of her own.

In planning a trip with a baby, first of all, be realistic. A young infant can be kept safe and healthy in a campground, for example, but without indoor conveniences, routine baby-care tasks may dominate your vacation. Second, anticipate what your needs will be at the destination. You should find out in advance if your hosts or hotels have any sort of bed for the child. A blanket-lined drawer or inflatable wading pool will do in a pinch, but it is better to arrange for a portable crib.

Small items like a bottle warmer for heating up formula, or a food grinder that you can take into restaurants, will make feedings much easier. And remember that while many babies love the beach, their

skin cannot tolerate more than a few minutes of exposure to the sun. Bring a hat, shirt and a beach umbrella, and keep the baby coated with full-strength sunscreen.

If you are traveling a long distance by car or train, plan ahead to combat restlessness. Stop the car for a stretch or get your baby out of the train seat from time to time to relieve the discomfort of sitting still, and bring an assortment of toys that you can use to distract her. On driving trips, you may also want to bring a picnic cooler for roadside snacks.

Air travel, while more confining, has the advantage of getting you where you are going much faster — and your baby travels free as long as she sits on your lap. Better yet, agents of most airlines will place you next to an empty seat if they have one available; therefore, you should be sure to let airline personnel know ahead of time that you will be traveling with an infant.

Leaving your baby at home

While your natural instincts will probably be to lavish your newborn with constant attention and affection, you will find that you cannot possibly do everything you need or want to do if you keep the baby with you all the time. Finding experienced, reliable baby-sitters will permit you to enjoy essential breaks from parental demands.

For most new parents, time away from the baby is limited to occasional nights out — for a quiet dinner, a movie or perhaps a hands-free shopping trip. Whatever the occasion, your first time away is usually a landmark event, often fraught with anxiety and uncertainty. Some new parents are skeptical about letting anyone else look after their baby, worrying that any separation will leave the child feeling abandoned and unloved.

Such separation anxieties are one-sided, however. For the first six months, at least, babies are not terribly upset by the absence of their parents; as long as they are kept warm and dry and are fed and cuddled on demand, they are usually quite content with a temporary substitute. Even after the baby is old enough to experience worries of her own, her distress will most likely be short-lived when you depart, if she is in the arms of a competent baby-sitter.

New-parent anxieties are very real, nevertheless, and they must be dealt with. The key to allaying your fears lies in finding the right person to take care of your baby and then in making sure that you take the time to prepare the sitter to handle both routine tasks and any emergencies that may arise *(box, opposite).*

Finding competent sitters

Experienced mothers normally use the networking approach to maintain their list of eligible baby-sitting candidates. But new parents are often unaware of the many places that reliable caregivers can be found and may feel they do not know where to begin. Apart from carefully checking references and qualifications, there are few hard and fast rules to apply to the search. Parents who are lucky enough to have relatives living nearby often have a source of loving — and free — child

When You Leave a Baby-Sitter in Charge

In your absence, a sitter assumes all of your responsibilities and most of your rights. The following guidelines will help to reduce uncertainties for you, your baby and your stand-in:

- Invite your sitter over in advance for a get-acquainted session.

- Take the baby-sitter on a house tour, pointing out door locks, fuse boxes, water shutoffs, fire alarms and fire extinguishers.

- Post an emergency telephone list — including a number where you

or a reliable neighbor can be reached. Also write down your home address for quick reference in the event of emergency.

- Demonstrate the procedures for feeding your baby and leave written instructions as well. Make sure that the baby-sitter knows whether the child is to be given water or fruit juice between feedings. Prepare bottles in advance.

- Leave a written list of rules covering your sitter's use of household equipment such as the television and

stereo. Prepare a snack or point out which foods she may use.

- Make it clear to the sitter that you do not permit visitors and that you expect the telephone to be kept free for your check-in calls.

- Point out essential baby supplies: diapers, pacifiers, security blankets.

- Make your baby-sitter aware of your child's likes and dislikes: tricks to make her stop crying, favorite ways to be held or burped, cherished toys and bedtime routines.

care available on short notice. Take care, however, not to abuse this privilege through overuse.

When it is necessary to hire a stranger to baby-sit, some parents feel confident leaving their newborn only with an experienced adult. Such sitters may be located through professional child-care agencies, local churches or senior citizen organizations.

Some neighborhoods have baby-sitting cooperatives in which parents baby-sit in one another's homes by prearrangement. You may also want to post notices or call officials at nearby schools or universities to find baby-sitters; married student couples, in particular, may possess the right balance of maturity and sensitivity to leave you at ease for your night out.

Teen-age baby-sitters
Neighborhood teenagers also represent a convenient pool of potential baby-sitters. Ask friends, work colleagues and other parents in the neighborhood for recommendations. You will feel most at ease if you know the families of the young people you hire to baby-sit for your child, or at least if you have been assured by someone you know well that the sitter is experienced and does a responsible job. Seek out candidates who have taken a baby-sitting course; such instruction is often available through the local Red Cross chapter or other organizations.

Parents generally find that the most stable age range for teen-age sitters is 12 to 15 years old. Younger children usually lack the maturity and judgment to care for a baby, and beyond 15, teenagers' priorities tend to change as their social lives become more active.

Wherever you may locate a caregiver, it is critical to heed your instinctive reactions to the person's character and personal style: If you have any reservations about a sitter, your evening out will likely be marred by nagging feelings of doubt and guilt. And if you are not happy with the person, chances are your baby will not be either. Respect the child's preferences in sitters; like adults, babies take to some people much better than others.

And by all means, once you find good sitters, treat them well. Pick them up punctually and get them home by the agreed-upon time. Discuss hourly wages in advance and be prepared to pay them in cash. If you cancel your plans at the last minute, pay the sitter for the evening's time anyway; that way the person will be more inclined to sit for you the next time you call. ❖

Feeding

Parents worry more about feeding their infants than about any other aspect of baby care. And most of the worry is unwarranted. Of course, a child's growth and development are inextricably tied to good nutrition, but babies are rarely malnourished as long as they are offered the proper foods and allowed to eat until satisfied.

A baby's natural instincts usually tell her when she is hungry and when that hunger has been satiated, and a hungry child will communicate that condition to you in no uncertain terms. If your baby wants more food than you have given her, she may cry and reach toward the empty spoon, or she may wake up fussing soon after a feeding. If she has eaten to contentment, she may turn away from the breast or bottle, clamp her lips together or bat away the hand holding the spoonful of food. By following such cues from your baby, you can relax and feel confident that she is being properly nourished according to her individual needs.

Sometimes, however, parents inadvertently create just the situation they fear — poor eating habits — by displaying anxiety at feeding time. Rushing a feeding along or becoming tense about the baby's performance at breast or bottle or about spills, spat-out food or a sticky high-chair tray creates stress the child can sense. She may respond by fussing, crying and not eating well, which can set a vicious cycle in motion.

Feeding an infant from your breast or a bottle or coping with an older baby who is learning to feed herself can be a time-consuming business, especially if your child is difficult about eating. It is important that you remain calm and take your time. Your child is learning important new skills, and as she moves on to each new stage of feeding you should continue to let her set the pace. Allowing your baby to taste new foods or try out new utensils without pressure gives her time to become acquainted and comfortable with them and helps make feeding time an adventure rather than a struggle.

Nourishment for the First Year

The question of whether it is better to breast-feed or bottle-feed a baby has been debated for decades. Today, most doctors recommend breast-feeding if the mother is so inclined, since breast milk has several health advantages over formula. But mothers who choose bottle-feeding can feel confident that their babies are receiving the nutrition necessary for growth and development.

Breast milk: nature's food

Human milk is the ideal food for human infants. It is naturally endowed with water, protein, carbohydrates, cholesterol, fat, vitamins and minerals in the correct proportions and in an easily digestible form. Breast-fed infants are rarely constipated, spit up less often and are less prone to gas problems than are bottle-fed babies. In addition, breast milk contains antibodies from the mother that give the baby immunity to many diseases; this is significant since the infant's own immune system does not function fully until about six months of age. And breast-fed infants are less likely to develop food allergies than are formula-fed infants.

Formulas to mimic mother's milk

Considering the benefits, it is little wonder that makers of commercial infant formulas attempt to simulate breast milk. Most formulas are based on soy protein or highly modified cow's milk. The modifications are needed because untreated cow's milk contains about four times the protein of breast milk, in types that are difficult for an infant to digest. The butterfat of cow's milk also poses digestion problems for babies, the carbohydrate content is lower than that of breast milk, and the vitamins and minerals are not balanced for a growing infant's needs. To compensate, formula makers reduce the protein content of cow's milk, substitute vegetable oils for butterfat, add carbohydrates and fortify the formula with vitamins and minerals. The result is nutritionally comparable to breast milk, although it lacks the protective antibodies.

Vitamin and mineral supplements

Infants receiving a commercial formula usually do not need vitamin and mineral supplements. Breast-fed infants, however, may require extra vitamin D since breast milk is relatively low in that vitamin. While vitamin D deficiency is rare among breast-fed babies, many doctors prescribe the supplement as a precaution.

Babies take on stores of iron from their mothers while in the womb, but at about four to six months of age, both breast-fed and bottle-fed infants begin to run short of the mineral. Doctors usually prescribe an iron supplement for breast-fed babies, replacing it with an iron-fortified cereal once the infant begins eating solid foods. A switch to an iron-fortified formula and the later addition of a cereal containing iron will solve the problem for bottle-fed babies. Check with your doctor, however, before making any changes in your baby's diet, and never give the child vitamin or mineral supplements without a doctor's supervision.

Overfeeding and underfeeding

Generally, newborns consume two to three ounces of food every two to four hours. By three to four months of age, infants feed less often but take in greater amounts — about 28 ounces a day in five or six feedings, although the amount consumed will vary with each baby. Babies regulate their food intake naturally and should be permitted to eat until they are satisfied. Letting your baby have some control over how much he eats will help avoid the problem of overfeeding.

Overfeeding occurs most often in bottle-fed babies. It can happen when you induce your baby to finish every drop of his formula, even when he seems not to want it. Overfeeding can also be caused by making the formula too strong. Follow the directions precisely when mixing a powdered or concentrated formula. Putting in too much powder or concentrate can result in a mix that has too many calories. And far from encouraging your baby's healthy growth, extra calories simply add fat to his body.

If, on the other hand, your infant consistently drains bottles of carefully prepared formula and remains fretful and upset, he may still be hungry. In that case, offer him more. Breast-fed infants, also, may eat too little, since it is difficult for you to gauge how much milk the infant has consumed. If you observe at any time that your baby is not gaining weight as he should or is becoming overweight in proportion to his length, consult your doctor for advice. Never decide on your own to adjust the composition of your child's formula to control his weight.

Growth patterns If your baby seems contented most of the time and is growing noticeably, you can be reasonably sure he is properly nourished. If you need confirmation, however, weigh your baby each week. Most babies add about six to eight ounces per week and grow about three quarters of an inch per month for the first three months of life. For the next three months, growth remains steady but weight gain usually slows to about five or six ounces a week. And for the second six months of life, babies add roughly two to three ounces per week and grow one-half inch per month. These figures, of course, are only averages. When examining your child, the doctor will look for consistent growth with weight proportionate to height, not adherence to a particular schedule.

Starting solid food The nutritional needs of an infant change little during the first four to six months of life; breast milk or formula provides all the nourishment a young baby needs. But as the child gets older, the amount of milk and type of food the baby consumes will change.

Between the ages of four and six months, your baby is becoming physiologically ready to receive solid foods: Her chewing and swallowing muscles are developing and her digestive system is beginning to mature. You will start feeding her solid foods gradually *(pages 78-83)*. As you add calories and nutrients to her diet through solid foods, she may have somewhat less of an appetite for breast milk or formula.

At about one year of age, when most of your baby's nourishment comes from solid foods, you can switch your child from breast milk or formula to whole cow's milk. By this time her milk intake will be reduced to about 16 to 24 ounces a day, and her digestive system will be mature enough to handle all the proteins in cow's milk.

Breast or Bottle: What's Best for You?

The nutritional and health merits of breast-feeding and bottle-feeding, as discussed on the preceding two pages, are important factors in deciding how to nourish your baby. But your own needs and inclinations are also important factors, since babies can thrive on either breast milk or formula. You should be comfortable with your feeding choice.

The convenience of breast-feeding

Both methods of feeding have their pros and cons. Generally, mothers who breast-feed appreciate its convenience. The milk is available whenever the baby is hungry, and no preparation is required before the feeding. Night feedings are as simple as collecting the baby and settling comfortably into a rocking chair.

Breast-feeding can also have physical advantages for mothers. Hormones stimulated by breast-feeding induce strong contractions of the uterus in the first week after delivery, returning it more quickly to its prepregnancy state. Nursing mothers also tend to return to their normal weight more quickly than their bottle-feeding counterparts since fat deposited during pregnancy is utilized for milk production.

On the other hand, breast-feeding means being careful about what you eat and drink. You should maintain a balanced diet, and since everything you consume will be transmitted to your baby through your milk, you should limit your intake of caffeine and alcohol. Consult your doctor before taking any drugs, even aspirin or a laxative.

In addition, many active women find it difficult to take 20 or 30 minutes every few hours to sit down and nurse the child themselves. Mothers with jobs outside the home may find it impossible — although they can still breast-feed by expressing milk for the feedings they will miss *(page 68)*. Even mothers without outside employment may feel that breast-feeding ties them too closely to their homes, particularly if they are reluctant to breast-feed in front of others.

The freedom of bottle-feeding

The greatest advantage of bottle-feeding is that it gives a mother more mobility. It is easier for her to return to work or to leave the baby with a sitter. The bottle-feeding mother also will be able to eat and drink as she likes and take medication without affecting the baby. Furthermore, the father can play a larger role and enjoy the closeness shared between the baby and the provider of nourishment. Relatives or older children can also develop their own bonds with the baby — and relieve a tired mom — by occasionally helping with feedings.

Of course, bottle-feeding involves carefully measuring and mixing formula, sterilizing bottles and nipples and warming bottles. If you travel, both the equipment and the process can be awkward. Formula, especially the convenient, premixed kind, is also expensive.

A third possibility is to combine breast- and bottle-feeding. Once a mother's breast milk is established — after about two to three weeks of breast-feeding — she can either express breast milk for bottles or supplement her milk with one or two bottles of formula a day. This solution may help the mother return to a job or leave the baby in someone else's care, and it lets the father participate in feedings. •:•

In Praise of Breast and Bottle

66 When my first baby was born 16 years ago, I just assumed I would bottle-feed; that was what the doctor recommended. I tried nursing the baby while I was in the hospital, but no one showed me how. When my last child was born, however, breast-feeding was in vogue and I was determined to try it. I nursed my daughter for 14 months, and it could not have been better. You feel such a life line to the baby's emotional well-being. 99

66 I tried both, and bottle-feeding, for me, was more difficult than breast-feeding. The first few months with a new baby can be an emotional roller coaster, and I did not need the nuisance of making bottles and worrying about whether they were sterile. The equipment gave me problems, too: Sometimes the holes in the nipples would be too big and the baby would swallow air, or the holes would be too small and the baby could not get enough formula. 99

66 I did not feel shut out when my wife breast-fed our son. I helped by bringing the baby to her in the middle of the night for feedings. If I had stayed in bed, I probably would have felt like an outsider. My wife was not producing enough milk, though, so after six weeks we switched to bottle-feeding. I enjoyed sharing in the baby's feedings and took pride in being able to take care of him in the middle of the night. When you first wake up, you regret having to get out of bed, but when you are sitting in the dark in the rocking chair, just the two of you, and the baby holds your thumb or pulls on the bottle, you feel great. It is a very special time. 99

66 I am a nurse, and I believe that breast-feeding is best for babies. I breast-fed my baby until my mother became ill and needed looking after; then I switched to formula. Although I felt guilty at the time, I know now that bottle-feeding is fine for babies — my baby is as healthy as can be. Mothers should choose the method of feeding that is best for them as individuals. When I am working in the hospital, I see new mothers all the time. Some of them do not really want to breast-feed, but do so because they are under pressure from their husbands or relatives. Others want to breast-feed, but do not have the confidence. I try to encourage them, but if they are not making this decision for themselves or do not have support at home, they can have a hard time of it. 99

66 I nursed my first baby just two months before the doctor determined that the baby was not getting enough milk and advised placing him on a bottle. Because I had not nursed my son as long as I wanted to, I ended up nursing my second baby too long — for 11 months — and it made me feel very confined. So when our third child came along, I decided to bottle-feed her. This way my husband and the older children can help feed the baby, and they love it. 99

66 I did not have any problems nursing either of my children. I feel confident about nursing, and I think the baby senses it — she's so calm and easy. Confidence probably has a lot to do with successful breast-feeding. My friend was sure she would not be able to breast-feed, and it turned out to be a self-fulfilling prophecy. My mother tried to breast-feed me, but the doctor insisted she weigh me after every feeding. She got so nervous, she finally gave up. 99

66 For me, the main problem with nursing was not having someone who could help me at the beginning, to show me how to keep my nipples from getting sore and so forth. 99

66 What amazes me about breast-feeding is the way the baby becomes a part of you. The physical closeness is so strong. You notice every little roll of their fat and feel so proud. 99

66 I was a breast-feeding dropout — not just once, but twice. Before my daughter was born I read everything I could get my hands on and thought I knew all there was to know about the subject. I plunged into breast-feeding like a great adventurer, and it all went fine for the first week or two. But as time went on, it got more difficult instead of easier. She seemed to need milk faster than I could produce it. She would begin crying two hours after her last feeding, and my milk glands just could not produce enough in that time. That made me anxious, and being anxious made me even more anxious, because I knew anxiety was a no-no for breast-feeding mothers. I began giving her supplemental bottles, and my milk supply dwindled faster than ever. After six weeks, I had to switch to bottle-feeding full time. When my son was born a couple of years later, I figured I knew all the pitfalls and could handle it this time, but again, I did not have enough milk and could not stop worrying about his needs. At the end of six weeks my milk was all gone. But I can honestly say that both of my children took right to the bottle and did not seem to mind the switch a bit. 99

Breast-Feeding

Many women find breast-feeding to be one of the greatest pleasures of early parenthood, providing unmatched moments of serenity and fulfillment. Initial attempts at breast-feeding, however, often leave first-time mothers feeling awkward and bewildered. These feelings usually can be overcome by the new mother with some basic information and a few simple techniques.

The making of milk

Breast milk is produced in clusters of tiny individual glands called alveoli. Small ducts carry the milk to an area behind the areola, the dark ring surrounding the nipple, where they enlarge to form collecting sinuses, or milk reserves. The baby squeezes these sinuses as she nurses, causing the nipple to elongate and the milk to come squirting through small duct openings.

When a baby is born, the clusters of tiny milk glands, called alveoli, in the mother's breasts *(below)* contain only colostrum, which is a sticky, protein-rich substance loaded with antibodies that protect the baby against infections. True milk begins to form in the breasts only a day or two later.

The pressure of the sucking baby's mouth on the areola, the dark pigmented area that surrounds the nipple, unleashes the hormone oxytocin, which in turn forces milk to travel downward from the milk glands to the nipple. This so-called "let down" of milk may be felt by the mother as a tingling sensation in her breasts. Sometimes, the mere sight or sound of her infant will trigger the let-down reflex in a nursing mother.

Suckling also stimulates the release of a second hormone, called prolactin, which causes the production of milk. Because milk is produced in the milk glands and not in the fatty tissue around them, a woman's breast size has nothing to do with how much milk she can produce. The amount of milk is instead a result of how much the baby nurses. The more often a mother nurses her baby, the more milk she will produce.

Getting a good start

Because your milk production depends on how much your baby nurses, it is important to get an early start with breast-feeding to ensure a good supply of milk. Many mothers nurse their babies right on the delivery table. And you should let your infant suckle as often as possible during the first days and weeks after birth.

Make sure to suckle your newborn on both breasts at each feeding, offering the second only when the baby finishes the first. Because newborns often satisfy their appetites before emptying the second breast, begin each subsequent feeding on the last breast that was sucked. Even if your milk is slow to come in at first, your infant's suckling will eventually stimulate its production. If you must be separated from your baby during a feeding time, you should express milk from your breasts, ei-

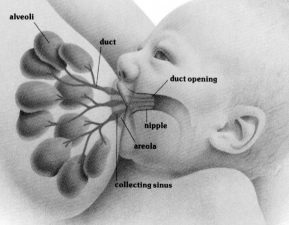

alveoli

duct

duct opening

nipple

areola

collecting sinus

ther by hand or with a special breast pump *(page 68)*, in order to keep your milk production up and to relieve the discomfort of breasts engorged with milk.

Breast-fed newborn babies usually want to be fed about every two hours, for a total of eight to 10 feedings a day. By the time they are two months old, they usually feed about every four hours. At three months, most babies sleep for six to seven hours after a late evening meal and need to be nursed only five times a day. Each baby's feeding pattern is different, however, so you should follow your baby's lead when breast-feeding.

Because breast-feeding mothers cannot watch their breasts empty as they could a bottle, many worry that their babies are not receiving enough nourishment. These worries are usually unfounded. If your baby has six to eight wet diapers each day (an indication that he is receiving sufficient fluid), is increasing in weight, has good skin tone and generally acts content, he is most likely getting all the nourishment he needs from breast milk.

The problem. *An inverted nipple (above) does not protrude far enough for the baby to suckle properly.*

Care for the mother Breast-feeding mothers need plenty of rest and a well-balanced diet rich in iron and calcium. To avoid dehydration, drink liquids such as water, milk and fruit juices whenever you are thirsty. But do not force down extra liquids when you are not thirsty.

Because many chemicals can make their way into your baby's system through your milk, you should avoid using certain drugs while breast-feeding, including cold medicines, antihistamines and nicotine. There is no evidence that moderate use of alcohol or caffeine is harmful to the infant while breast-feeding. Many physicians, in fact, recommend having a glass of wine or beer to relax the nursing mother. But be sure to discuss with your doctor any use of alcohol, caffeine or over-the-counter medication.

Reminders for Nursing Mothers

- Feed your baby on demand; as long as the infant is thriving, you should never try to force an arbitrary feeding schedule on him.

- Do not use birth-control pills — which can reduce your milk supply — until you are ready to wean. But do not fall victim to the mistaken notion that a nursing mother cannot conceive *(page 71)*.

- To keep milk from wetting and staining clothes, line your bra with disposable pads or wear a special nursing bra. Be sure your bras fit well; a bra that is too tight can cause milk ducts to clog and become infected.

- For privacy when you are nursing in public, carry a receiving blanket that can be discreetly draped over your shoulder and breast.

- Smile and talk or sing softly to your baby while you nurse him. The child will soon begin to associate your face and the sound of your voice with the pleasure and comfort that he receives from feeding.

Two remedies. *You may correct an inverted nipple by wearing a plastic breast shield (top) under your bra for a few hours a day during pregnancy. The shield will encourage the nipple to protrude through a central opening. A snap-on cover protects the nipple. Or you can try a special exercise: Press the base of the nipple gently (bottom) to help it become more erect.*

The Art of Relaxed Nursing

The nervousness or discomfort experienced by some new mothers during their baby's first breast-feedings can usually be overcome with practice and a few simple techniques. The procedures shown here will help you nurse without damaging tender nipples. The positions illustrated opposite will ensure that both you and your baby are relaxed and comfortable.

Before nursing, make sure that your arms and back are well supported to avoid strain, which can cause back pain and interfere with your milk flow. Also, make sure you are sitting or lying in a position that allows you to hold your baby level without having to lean over. Some well-placed pillows, such as under your baby while nursing in a chair, can help achieve this comfort.

To begin the breast-feeding session, cradle the baby close to your breast, then lightly stroke the corner of your baby's mouth with your finger. This will stimulate the baby to turn his head in search of a nipple — a reflexive response known as rooting. Gradually, the stroking will become unnecessary as your baby learns that the closeness of your bare breast means milk is nearby. When the baby takes the breast in his mouth, make sure his mouth covers a large area of the areola, since it is pressure on the areola, rather than sucking on the nipple, that stimulates the milk to flow. Do not allow him to chew on the nipple itself, which may cause soreness or cracking. If your milk comes out too quickly, causing the baby to choke, nurse with the child in a more upright position, or reduce the flow by pressing above and below the areola with your fingers while your baby suckles.

Starting the session. *To help your baby find your breast, place your fingers scissor-like around the breast and gently guide the nipple and the areola into his mouth.*

Helping the baby's breathing. *Pull your breast slightly away from your baby's nose so that he can breathe easily and comfortably while nursing. This is especially important at the beginning of a feeding, when the breasts are full.*

Removing the breast. *To end nursing, slip a fingertip into the corner of your baby's mouth. This will break the suction between the child's lips and your breast and allow you to pull your breast away without damaging the nipple.*

A horizontal position. *Although lying down may be a comfortable position for late-night nursing, some horizontal postures can slow your milk flow. To prevent this from occurring, make sure you are positioned so that the muscles under your arm are relaxed. Pillows can help absorb the weight of your head and back.*

An upright position. *To nurse while sitting, cradle your baby in your arm so that his head is slightly raised and his body is turned toward you. Be sure your back is well supported. Slipping a pillow behind your back or under the baby may provide more comfort.*

A Special-Purpose Nursing Position

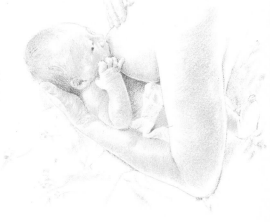

The football hold. *For women who have delivered by cesarean section, nursing the baby in a horizontal football hold (above) minimizes pressure on the surgical incision. With a pillow under your baby for support, hold him so that his upper back and head are cradled in your hand and his bottom rests near your elbow. Then lift him to your breast. The hold can be a boon to any busy mother, since it leaves one hand free.*

Expressing and Storing Mother's Milk

Expressing milk is a helpful technique for nursing mothers who must be separated from their babies during feeding times or whose babies reject a feeding due to an illness. A working mother, for example, can collect milk from her breasts and then store it for use when she is absent. Expressing milk also helps to keep milk production up during periods of missed feedings, and it can relieve the discomfort caused by engorged breasts.

Breast milk can be expressed either by hand or with a specially designed breast pump. Hand expression requires no equipment — other than containers for storing the milk — and involves simple techniques *(below)* that can be performed in the privacy of your home or office. It is, however, a time-consuming process, and not all mothers can successfully produce milk by hand.

Breast pumps range in design from small, hand-operated models that fit easily into a purse to bulky, electric-powered models that weigh as much as 25 pounds. While pumps are often more efficient than hand expression — and are less tiring for the mother to use — most doctors recommend their use only when really necessary. In choosing a breast pump, you should consider such factors as cost, portability and ease of cleaning or sterilizing. Ask your physician if certain designs are likely to irritate or damage already-sore breasts and nipples. And remember that even the most

efficient model cannot duplicate the unique physical and emotional experience of your infant's suckling.

Manual pumps consist of a container for expressed milk, a plastic flange that fits over the nipple, and a device to create suction in the flange. The suction devices range from rubber bulbs, similar to those on bicycle horns, to telescoping plastic cylinders that move up and down like a piston. While both types are lightweight and easily transportable, pumps with rubber parts may require special cleaning to remove milk residues that adhere to gaskets or leak into suction bulbs.

Although electric pumps are more complex and expensive, their efficiency in emptying the breast is often preferred by mothers who must express milk regularly throughout the day. Some models may be rented from pharmacies and medical-supply houses, and most come with an array of useful accessories, including measuring cups and bottles for storing your milk.

Although breast milk can be expressed at any hour, the best time is in the morning when your breasts are full or in the evening after the last feeding. Before beginning, wash your hands and sterilize any jars, pumps or other equipment you are using. Breast milk must be refrigerated immediately and can be stored in the refrigerator for 24 hours or in the freezer for up to three months.

Massaging the breast. *To push milk down the ducts, cup your breast in one hand; use the flat of the other hand to stroke downward toward the areola. Using several firm strokes in each position, work your way around the breast.*

Preparing to express. *Once the milk has begun to pool in the sinuses behind the areola, support the breast in the palm of your hand and place your thumb about an inch above the areola. Then firmly run your thumb down the breast to the areola.*

Collecting the milk. *Press your thumb in and up on the areola, taking care not to block the ducts by squeezing the nipple. Collect the milk in a sterilized container. Rotate around the areola so that milk is expressed from all the sinuses.*

Care of the Nipples

Most breast-feeding mothers experience sore or cracked nipples, especially in the first few days of nursing. Usually, the soreness goes away within a few days. In other cases, however, such as when a nursing baby's mouth is not properly enclosing the nipple and areola, the pain may be sufficient to discourage a mother from breast-feeding.

With proper care and cleaning of the nipples, you can usually avoid or minimize cracking and soreness due to the unaccustomed friction of your baby's initial suckling. To prevent soreness caused by improper placement of the baby on the breast, make sure that both the nipple and the areola are well into your baby's mouth when she suckles. Also, avoid a painful and potentially damaging tug-of-war when trying to remove your baby from your breast. Either wait for the child to stop suckling or gently break the suction, as shown on page 66, before pulling your breast away.

Keeping nipples clean and dry

Because breasts frequently leak, creating damp areas in the bra that chafe and irritate the nipple, line your bra with cotton breast pads and replace them promptly when moist. To improve drying, expose your nipples to air whenever possible; if you are wearing a nursing bra, leave the flaps open when in the privacy of your home. Rinse your nipples frequently *(below)* to remove milk residues. Never use soap, which can dry and crack the skin. And never scrub the nipples, since this will wear away the natural oils that protect the skin.

Treating sore nipples

If one of your nipples becomes painful during breast-feeding, you may wish to stop nursing on that breast until it heals. Lubricate the sore nipple with lanolin; do not use any creams or lotions that might clog the pores. Express milk from the affected breast while you continue to nurse with the other one. Some mothers nurse on the sore breast by placing the nipple farther back in the baby's mouth.

At least twice a day, wash your breasts with warm water, taking care to rinse off milk residues, which can block the tiny milk-duct openings. Then pat the breast dry with a soft towel.

When Breast Problems Arise

Occasionally, a physical problem will develop in a breast that may cause considerable pain and discomfort to the nursing mother. Quick attention to the problem can usually resolve it without requiring that breast-feeding be stopped.

Engorged breasts

When feedings are delayed or interrupted, or when let down does not occur, milk can back up within the milk ducts, causing the breasts to become firm, warm and tender to the touch. The skin may appear shiny; the nipples, flat and distended. This painful swelling of the breasts is known as engorgement.

The cure for engorgement is to get rid of the excess milk, either by nursing your baby longer and more frequently or by expressing milk from your breasts. Because the nipple becomes flat when a breast is engorged and is therefore difficult for your infant to suckle, you may need to hand-express some milk before offering your baby the breast. To encourage let down to occur, you could apply a warm compress to the breasts before nursing; a cold compress after nursing can help relieve any pain you experience.

Blocked ducts and infections

Sometimes, a milk duct becomes plugged with dried milk and dead cells, and milk backs up within it. The blocked area of the breast may become tender or form into a small, hard, painful lump. The plug should be treated as soon as possible to keep it from enlarging and becoming infected. Try nursing more frequently on the affected breast to work the plug loose. In addition, apply a warm, moist compress to the tender area of the breast and then use gentle manual massage, which usually dissolves the plug.

If you observe no improvement, see your doctor: A plugged duct that goes untreated can lead to a breast infection called mastitis. A breast can also become infected when bacteria, such as the staphylococcus, enter through cracks in the nipple. An infected breast turns red and feels hot and tender to the touch. The mother usually develops a fever and flulike symptoms, such as nausea and a general aching. In rare cases, an abscess, or collection of pus, will form at the site of the infection.

Breast infections most often occur when a mother becomes over-tired or when her nursing schedule is abruptly changed. If you suspect that your breast has become infected, or if fever or flulike symptoms develop, you should contact your physician. Treatment includes complete bed rest and keeping the breast empty of milk; antibiotics may also be prescribed. You can usually continue to breast-feed your baby while suffering from a breast infection. Some physicians, however, recommend that if antibiotics are being used, a mother should temporarily wean her baby to prevent the child from ingesting large doses of the medication along with the milk. If you must stop breast-feeding your infant for a few days, be sure to express milk frequently *(page 68)* until you are able to resume nursing. Applying heat to the sore area may also provide relief. ⋰

About Breast-Feeding

My doctor says there is a strong chance my baby will be born prematurely. Will I still be able to breast-feed?

Yes. Because of the special antibodies found in breast milk, many doctors strongly advise mothers of premature babies to breast-feed. In fact, the milk of premature babies' mothers has a different composition than that of full-term mothers. Perhaps nature has designed the premie's mother's milk to serve her baby's special needs. Since you will probably be discharged from the hospital before your baby, express and store your breast milk *(page 68)* so hospital staff can feed your baby when you cannot be present.

My husband and I are going to be adopting an infant soon. I've heard that some adoptive mothers breast-feed their babies. Is this possible?

A small percentage of women can successfully fool their bodies into producing milk for adopted babies, usually by using a breast pump for many weeks before the baby arrives. Many adoptive mothers, however, receive too little advance notice to induce milk production. Even when there is adequate warning, these efforts produce uncertain amounts of milk and the baby must receive formula for the bulk of his diet. But even if you cannot produce milk, suckling an adopted baby may contribute to the critical bonding process.

When I breast-feed my new baby, his older sister gets very jealous. How can I help her overcome these feelings?

One of the advantages of breast-feeding is that you have a free arm to wrap around another child. Encourage your daughter to sit next to you while you breast-feed; ask her to bring a book for you to read to her. Also, be sure to plan activities with your daughter when you can be away from the baby.

A friend once told me that I won't get pregnant as long as I breast-feed. Is this really true?

No. Breast-feeding mothers have only a slightly lower chance of conceiving than those who bottle-feed. Although a

nursing mother may not menstruate for two to 18 months after the birth of her baby, she may still be ovulating during that time; the lack of menstrual blood may be due to hormonal changes.

My baby is acting fussy and seems to want to nurse all the time. How can I tell if I am producing enough milk?

Your baby is most likely experiencing a growth spurt. All babies have several episodes of sudden growth during their first few months. To satisfy your baby's need for more food, let him nurse as frequently as he wants. Within a few days your milk supply should increase to meet your baby's needs.

My six-month-old baby occasionally bites me while nursing. What can I do to stop this behavior?

Your baby's biting may be the result of teething. Try rubbing ice or a cold cloth on her gums before or during breast-feeding to relieve the soreness. Some babies bite as they fall asleep and close their jaws. This can be prevented by taking your baby off the breast as soon as she has finished eating. When your baby bites, say "No" firmly and remove her temporarily from the breast; if she bites a second time, end the nursing session. Do not react too strongly, however, or the baby may associate nursing with your becoming upset.

My five-month-old baby has suddenly refused to have anything to do with breast-feeding. I would like to continue nursing but wonder if it wouldn't be better just to wean the child to a bottle.

Occasionally, a baby — usually one between the ages of four and eight months — will go on a nursing strike for several days. The precise reason for this rejection of the breast is often unclear, but sometimes refusals occur during teething, when frequent stuffy noses and blocked sinuses make nursing difficult for the baby. As the child's congestion diminishes, he may be encouraged to try the nipple again. Meanwhile, be sure to express milk to keep your supply up. Feed this milk in bottles to your baby, or supplement the child's feedings with formula.

Bottle-Feeding

Parents who want to bottle-feed their babies are confronted by a variety of formulas and bottle types. What you choose depends mainly on your own priorities of convenience and economy, because all the commercial formulas are nutritionally complete, and every bottle does the job.

Kinds of formulas

Infant formulas come in three forms: powder, liquid concentrate and ready-to-use liquid. Powdered formulas are the cheapest, lightest and easiest to store. However, they require the most work because you must measure the powder precisely and mix it with boiled, carefully measured tap water. Concentrates are more expensive, but easier to mix. They also require sterilized tap water, however. Most expensive and most convenient are the premixed formulas, which can be poured directly into the bottle. Some premixed brands can even be bought already sealed into sterile disposable bottles. Because they provide a good breeding ground for bacteria, both concentrates and premixed formulas must be refrigerated and used within 48 hours once they are opened. A box of powdered formula can be kept in a cool, dry place for up to one month after it is opened.

Types of bottles

You have a choice of glass or rigid plastic bottles or disposable plastic sacks that fit into a rigid plastic holder. Glass bottles are the simplest to clean, will not scratch easily and can take the heat of a dishwasher or microwave oven. Unfortunately, they are breakable. Plastic bottles will not break and they weigh less than glass, but they may be harder to sterilize, because they scratch and stain easily; scratches can harbor germs. Disposable plastic sacks eliminate the need for sterilizing. They are expensive, however, and you might have difficulty measuring the amount of liquid inside them.

Even the bottle nipple has its variations. Some come in different hole sizes to accommodate different liquids (milk, water and juice, for example). Some have a so-called "orthodontic" shape, designed to conform to the baby's palate. You might want to try out several kinds to find the one your baby prefers.

You probably will need 10 to 12 eight-ounce bottles to accommodate six or eight feedings a day. (The extras are in case you break or lose a few.) Buy the same number of nipples, screw rings and bottle covers or caps. Bottle and nipple brushes are required for cleaning. For mixing formula, you should have a large, covered measuring cup or covered pitcher, a funnel and a long-handled sterile spoon.

Keeping formula sterile

Because a bottle-fed infant does not receive protective antibodies from his mother's milk, his immune system is fragile at first, so you must be particularly careful about keeping his formula and bottles sterile. Warm formula is an ideal growth medium for germs. Do not keep a bottle at room temperature for longer than an hour, or a half hour in hot weather. Discard any formula left in the bottle after a feeding. When traveling, use ready-mixed liquid formula, or else carry your baby's bottles of formula ice-cold in an insulated container, with a separate thermos of

While all nipples fasten with screw rings, they come in various shapes, including the traditional rounded form (top) and an orthodontic shape suiting the contours of the palate (second from top).

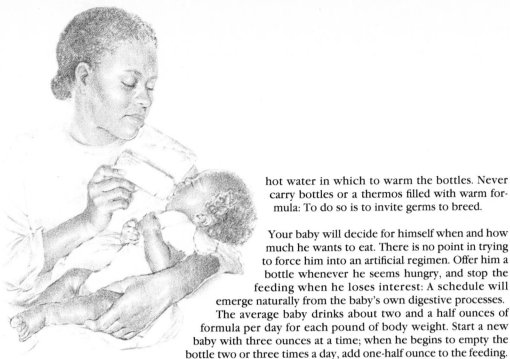

hot water in which to warm the bottles. Never carry bottles or a thermos filled with warm formula: To do so is to invite germs to breed.

Your baby will decide for himself when and how much he wants to eat. There is no point in trying to force him into an artificial regimen. Offer him a bottle whenever he seems hungry, and stop the feeding when he loses interest: A schedule will emerge naturally from the baby's own digestive processes. The average baby drinks about two and a half ounces of formula per day for each pound of body weight. Start a new baby with three ounces at a time; when he begins to empty the bottle two or three times a day, add one-half ounce to the feeding.

Classic feeding position. *Cradle your baby, head and upper body slightly elevated, in the crook of one arm while holding the bottle in your other hand.*

When you are bottle-feeding your child, your attention to such details as the temperature of the formula, size of the nipple hole and even the angle at which the bottle is held can make the difference between a successful and a frustrating experience. Cold formula will not harm a baby, but your child may prefer it lukewarm. If so, warm it for a few minutes in hot water or in a microwave oven on a low setting. Be very careful if you use a microwave; the formula can become scalding hot while the bottle remains cool. Always test the temperature of warmed formula with the classic technique: Shake out a few drops on the inside of your wrist, where it should feel just slightly warmer than your skin.

While you are doing this, observe the flow of formula from the nipple. It should emerge in a steady procession of drops. If it comes out too slowly, the baby may get tired of sucking and also may take in a lot of air. If the flow is too fast, the child may thrust his tongue against the nipple to slow it down, which can hinder later tooth development. Throw away any nipples with holes that are too large. If you like, you can enlarge holes that are too small: Push the blunt end of a needle into a cork and heat the other end until it is red hot. Holding the cork so as not to burn your fingers, insert the hot needle into the nipple hole to melt the hole's edges and enlarge the opening.

To begin feeding, place your baby in a suitable position *(above left and below right)* and gently stroke a corner of his mouth with your finger. He will turn reflexively toward the finger and search for the nipple with his mouth. Hold the bottle firmly when he takes it in his mouth and position it to keep the neck filled with milk to avoid introducing air. Make sure that the baby is propped up a little, to prevent milk from running through his Eustachian tubes into his ears: This could lead to an ear infection. A steady stream of bubbles rising through the milk will tell you that your infant is feeding successfully.

Then sit back and relax. The average baby takes about 20 minutes to finish a bottle. ⁙

An eye-contact position. *So that your baby can look directly at you while he eats, rest him on your knees with his feet in the crook of your arm, and prop his head up with your hand.*

Steps to a Sterile Formula

Although tap water is potable in the United States, and formula is presterilized, many doctors still feel that baby formula and feeding equipment should be sterilized. The underdeveloped immune system of a young baby succumbs easily to germs that probably would not affect an older child, and scrupulous cleanliness can help to protect the infant. Although the sterilizing routine is time-consuming, you will soon get used to it. It will also take less time as your infant gets older and requires fewer feedings.

The first step in sterilizing bottles is to make sure that your hands and countertops are clean. Make sure you have paper towels or just-washed dish towels on hand to dry your equipment.

After washing bottles and nipples, you can sterilize them in one of several ways. You can submerge them in a special sterilizing solution of cold water and sodium hypochlorite tablets. You can wash the bottles in the dishwasher (boiling the nipples separately). Or you can boil bottles and nipples in a rack in a large saucepan *(below)*. You can also boil the bottles after they have been filled with formula; this last technique is called terminal sterilization. If you use this system you must remember to leave the caps loose so that expanding air can escape as the bottles are heated. The bottles should be boiled for 25 minutes and allowed to cool at least one hour before you tighten the caps and store the bottles in the refrigerator.

If you use your dishwasher, simply run the bottles through on a normal setting. To extend the life of rubber nipples, boil them in a saucepan for five to 10 minutes instead of using your dishwasher. You should check nipples before each use by stretching them to detect cracks or nicks that could harbor germs. Nipples with a permanently sticky, gummy feel are ready to disintegrate and must be thrown away.

If you mix the formula from powder or liquid concentrate, the water you use must be sterilized by boiling for five to 10 minutes. Any equipment that you use in preparing the formula, such as a can opener, must also be sterilized with boiling water. Washing the equipment in warm, soapy water is not sufficient. When you fill the bottles with formula, close them either with inverted nipples and caps or with upright nipples protected by tall covers, and then refrigerate them immediately.

Many boiling racks hold eight bottles at a time. Since a newborn baby needs about seven feedings over a 24-hour period, you will need to sterilize and prepare bottles only once a day. And by the time your baby is about six months old, her resistance will be up to par. Then you will be able to stop the sterilization and rely on normal washing methods.

Boiling Bottles and Nipples

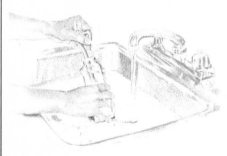  

Washing bottles and nipples. *First rinse the bottles with cold water. Then scrub bottles, rings and nipples with hot, soapy water and a bottle brush. Be sure to turn the nipples inside out and scrub their interiors as well.*

Sterilizing bottles. *Place the clean bottles in a rack in a pot of cold water. Bring the water to a boil, cover and boil for five to 10 minutes. Remove the bottles with sterile tongs. Let them cool for two hours before filling with formula.*

Sterilizing nipples. *Sterilize the nipples, screw rings and bottle caps or covers in boiling water in a covered saucepan — shown uncovered here so the contents can be seen. Boil for five to 10 minutes, then cool them on a clean surface.*

Preparing Formula from Liquid Concentrate

Opening the can. *Pour boiling water over the can to sterilize its exterior before you open it. Then use a sterilized can opener to punch openings in the can.*

Measuring the concentrate. *Use only the specified amount and measure the concentrate exactly by holding each bottle at eye level to check.*

Adding water. *Pour boiled, cooled water into each bottle to make the proper amount of formula. Cap the bottles, shake them until mixed and refrigerate them. Do not store mixed liquid concentrate formula for more than 48 hours.*

Preparing Powdered Formula

Measuring the water. *Pour the required amount of boiled, cooled water into a measuring cup or pitcher. Do not measure before boiling, because some water will be lost through evaporation.*

Adding the powder. *Using the scoop provided with the formula, add the required amount of powder to the water. Level each scoopful with a sterile knife. Stir the mixture until all the powder dissolves. Pour into sterilized bottles.*

Closing the bottles. *Fit the nipples on the bottles, either upright enclosed under tall covers, or inverted under flat bottle caps. Refrigerate the bottles at once. Do not store them longer than 24 hours.*

Common Concerns

About Bottle-Feeding

My baby can almost hold her bottle. Can I prop it up and let her finish alone?

No! This is a bad practice for several reasons. A baby left alone with a bottle could choke on the milk or on her own spit-up. Also, a baby who feeds lying down can develop an ear infection from milk dripping into the Eustachian tubes. And falling asleep with a bottle can lead to serious tooth decay later on, because the formula lingering in the mouth can provide a fertile breeding ground for germs.

My baby isn't gaining weight on his formula. What can I do?

First, be sure you are giving him enough to eat. Do not mix a stronger formula, but more formula. Put at least two ounces more than you think he will drink into each bottle. Then if he doesn't take much from his first bottle of the day, he can make up for it later. Don't be too strict about schedules; feed him when he is hungry, not when the clock dictates. Another problem could be the nipple. If the hole is too small, your baby may get tired of the effort of sucking and give up before he's really had enough formula. You can enlarge the hole yourself *(page 73)*.

Is it true that a baby fed on formula needs additional water to enable his kidneys to function properly?

As a routine, no. But it really depends on the climate in which you live. If it is very hot, your baby may need extra water to help his kidneys eliminate unusable proteins and salt. In this case, you should supplement his formula with bottles of water that have been boiled and then cooled. Formulas contain enough water for babies who live in moderate climates.

How will I know if my baby is allergic to cow's milk formula?

Common signs of milk intolerance include vomiting, diarrhea, rashes, cramps, coughing and colic. These symptoms should send you to a doctor for testing. If the physician decides your baby is allergic to cow's milk, she will probably advise switching to a soy-based formula.

I notice that all formulas contain sugar. I don't like the thought of giving my baby

sugar and would like to know if there is a sugar-free formula I can use.

The sugars in your baby's formula are carbohydrates that are vital for normal body function. They are not the same as the refined sugars and sweeteners you are rightly concerned about. Breast milk contains about 50 percent lactose, a sugar, and so does formula. Don't eliminate this; just don't add sweets later on.

Would it be better for my baby if I prepared my own homemade formula from evaporated milk?

No. Although it is less expensive, homemade formula based on evaporated milk is not as nutritious as commercial formula. It lacks certain vitamins, and it contains too much protein and minerals, which may put stress on an infant's kidneys.

When can I let my baby start drinking from a cup?

Cup drinking can be started around six months, although a baby should not have to give up completely the comfort and pleasure of his bottle before his first birthday. Let him alternate between bottle and cup for a few months. Don't pressure him. Even a toddler should be allowed a bottle once in a while if he wants it.

My baby is picky about taking her bottle. Is it possible that she doesn't like the taste of her formula?

Formulas do differ quite a lot in taste, so she might very well prefer another one. But it is rare that a brand of formula will keep a hungry baby from eating, so if your child refuses to eat altogether, she may have another problem. Ask your doctor's advice before switching to another brand.

Since we switched from breast- to bottle-feeding, my baby's stools have changed. Should I be concerned?

No. After your baby switches from breast milk to cow's milk formula, his stools normally become firmer and darker in color and have more of an adult fecal odor. Also, a formula-fed baby has bowel movements less frequently than a breast-fed one. A child on formula may develop constipation. If so, give him a bottle of cooled, boiled water once a day in addition to his regular feedings. Call your physician if the problem continues.

Burping and Spitting Up

Burping almost inevitably follows feeding in every infant's meal-time ritual. Both breast-fed and bottle-fed babies will swallow some air along with their milk; if they take in too much, the air will distend their stomachs, making them uncomfortable until it is expelled. Sometimes the baby spits up a little milk with the air. This is normal and will decrease when the infant is between the ages of seven and nine months.

You can help your baby by feeding him properly. Breast-fed babies generally have fewer problems. Bottle-fed babies swallow air more readily. To avoid that, hold the bottle at such an angle that the neck, not just the nipple, is completely filled with milk. You should check to make sure the hole of the nipple is open and large enough for milk. Some bottle-fed infants swallow air when sucking too hard at a blocked nipple.

You can also help your baby by burping him after feedings or when he sucks in so much air that he is too uncomfortable to continue. If he stops sucking for a moment, take advantage of this pause to burp him gently before resuming the feeding. Do not interrupt a happily feeding baby just to burp him, though.

Many babies, especially those past the age of two to three months, do not need to be burped until they have finished eating. When your baby is clearly finished, hold him in a burping position and rub or gently pat his back. A burp should come within about three minutes. If he does not burp, wait a few minutes and try again. Sometimes small quantities of air in a baby's stomach form tiny bubbles that cannot be burped up until they have collected into one large bubble. If he still does not burp, you can put him down for his nap. If he has to, he may burp on his own later while lying in his crib.

Over-the-shoulder burp. *Protect your shoulder with a cloth. Then hold the baby against your chest looking over your shoulder, and gently but firmly rub or pat the child's back until you hear him burp.*

Spitting up When a baby spits up, he is usually regurgitating a mixture of food and spittle from the top of his stomach. When this happens some time after a feeding, the digestive juices will have curdled the milk or formula, making it smell sour. Spitting up often happens when the baby has had too much milk; make sure that you are not feeding him more than he wants, and check the bottle nipple to see if the hole is too large, giving the baby too much too fast. Jiggling or bouncing the baby just after he has eaten can also bring up a recent meal.

Spitting up is not the same as vomiting, and it is not a sign of illness. In an infant, the muscles that control the passage between the stomach and the esophagus are immature, so the passage is often open and some spitting up is to be expected. If your baby is clearly vomiting — bringing up all the contents of his stomach — and especially if he is vomiting frequently, forcibly or has other symptoms of distress such as a fever or diarrhea, call your doctor. ❖

Horizontal burping. *Place the baby face down across your lap or on the bed, with a towel underneath his head, and rub or pat his back until he burps. If an infant is too young to hold up his head, turn his face to one side before burping him.*

Sitting upright. *Seat your baby on your lap; support his chin with a towel-covered hand. Gently pat his back until he burps.*

Weaning and Solid Foods

A two-handled mug with a spillproof lid and spout can help ease the child's transition from breast-feeding or bottle-feeding to drinking from an ordinary cup.

As your baby grows older, you will naturally begin to think about when and how to wean her from breast or bottle and introduce cup-feeding and solid foods. In general, it is best to wean a child over several weeks or months, letting her become gradually accustomed to these two big changes in her life: taking milk from a cup instead of a nipple, and eating meals composed mainly of solid foods rather than milk. Going at a slow pace, overlapping the old and the new, also helps the child better adjust to new food tastes and textures and to losing the comfort and security of sucking. And for breast-feeding mothers, gradual weaning can mean less discomfort from engorged breasts.

When to begin

There is no right age at which to start weaning a baby. Only you and your child can decide when is the best time to begin the process. Sometimes, the baby will signal that she is ready to begin by pulling away from the breast or bottle and showing more interest in foods eaten by other family members. Other times, of course, parents will decide to initiate weaning because of a factor such as a mother returning to work.

Most babies are ready to begin eating solid foods and drinking from a cup between the ages of four and six months. By then, a baby is physically able to swallow and digest solid foods, and he begins to need the more concentrated source of calories and nutrients that solids offer. Introducing solids at an earlier age is not recommended, because it could lead to several potential health difficulties for the baby, including dehydration and food-intolerance problems.

Giving up the nipple

While infants can usually begin to sample specially prepared solid foods between the ages of four and six months, most pediatricians believe that babies have a basic need to suck until they are one year old and advise against weaning a baby completely off a nipple — whether it be breast or bottle — before she reaches that age.

Just as there is no set age at which you must begin the weaning process, there is no set age at which your child should completely give up the breast or bottle. You may continue to breast-feed or give your child a bottle as long as both of you are comfortable doing so. Some parents extend the process of weaning from a nipple over many months, completing it only when their children reach two years of age, or even older.

Because it is an emotional as well as a physical adjustment for a child, weaning is best accomplished when she is experiencing no other stresses in her life. If your child is ill or teething, or if she is entering a new day-care setting or experiencing other changes in her daily routine, you should postpone the weaning process until she feels better or has settled into her new surroundings.

From breast to bottle

If you wish to wean your baby off breast milk before she is six months old, give her bottled formula until she is old enough to take other forms of nourishment.

To wean a child from the breast to a bottle, begin by selecting the

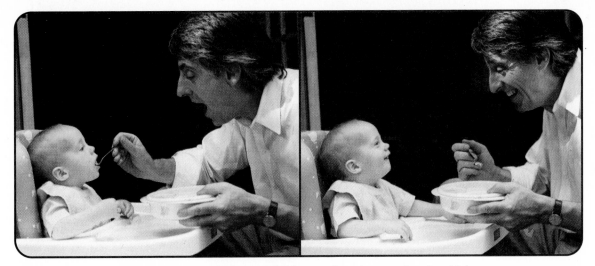

daily feeding in which your child seems least interested or in which your breasts are least full. Offer the child a bottle of formula in place of the breast. If your baby appears to dislike the new taste, try a mixture of half formula and half breast milk that you have expressed manually *(page 68)*. Once your child has grown accustomed to taking a bottle at one feeding, substitute the bottle at other feedings as well until she is completely weaned from the breast.

If you wean gradually, you should feel little discomfort from engorged breasts. Generally, milk production will begin to decline after a feeding is skipped two days in a row. If your breasts should become tender, try expressing some milk — but only enough to relieve the discomfort; otherwise, you may stimulate milk production. Reducing the amount of fluids you drink can also help keep the breasts from becoming too full. Occasionally, weaning can lead to a plugged duct and breast infection *(page 70)*. Contact your physician if areas of your breasts become sore or lumpy.

During weaning, many babies miss the special intimacy of breast-feeding. Be sure to provide your child with extra cuddling and attention during the weaning process to make up for this lost closeness. With planning, patience and plenty of love, this period of transition need not be traumatic for either you or your child.

Drinking from a cup To introduce your child to cup-feeding, choose a time when he is quiet and not too hungry — perhaps halfway through a breast- or bottle-feeding. Place a few teaspoons of formula or expressed breast milk into a cup and gently lift the cup's rim to your baby's lips. If he rejects the

Practical Tips for Easier Weaning

- Whether you are weaning from breast to bottle, bottle to cup, or liquids to solids, expect spills and spit-ups. Wear an apron and feed the baby in the kitchen, where messes can be easily cleaned.

- To ease the adjustment throughout the weaning period, gradually phase in any new method of feeding, using it only on alternate days at first.

- When weaning from breast to bottle, if your baby rejects one type of nipple, try another; a different shape or texture may be acceptable.

- Since babies are distracted by the smell of their mother's milk, have the father or grandparents give initial bottle feedings.

- If the baby screams continuously, let her nurse; try weaning again when she is less hungry or tired.

- If your baby rejects a bottle, try a feeding cup instead; she may accept the new shape and size of the cup.

- If you have nursed your baby in a particular rocking chair, hide the chair for a couple of weeks.

- To help your child make the transition from bottle to cup, do not let her walk around with a bottle or take one to bed.

- When introducing new solid foods to your baby, turn mealtime into a fun time, inventing and playing games with food and utensils.

- As your youngster reaches the finger-feeding stage, you should be prepared to let her make an even bigger mess with her food; exploring new foods absorbs her attention and satisfies her curiosity.

cup, simply try again at another feeding. Never force cup-feeding on a baby.

Once your child is drinking formula or breast milk from a cup, you may begin to serve him water or fruit juices from a cup as well. Always be sure to give your child natural fruit juices, not fruit drinks, which usually have a high sugar content that can harm a baby's developing teeth. Citrus juices, a common cause of allergies, should not be given to a child younger than 12 months. And whole cow's milk should not be given until the child is consuming two thirds of his calories as solid foods.

Once your child's teeth begin to come in, give him juice and cow's milk from a bottle only at meal-time — never as a pacifier between meals. When sucked from a bottle, the sugars in cow's milk and juice tend to concentrate in the mouth, which can cause cavities in young teeth.

To prevent accidents during meals, a child should always be strapped into a high chair before the tray is positioned and feeding begins.

Baby's first solid foods

Your baby's first solid foods should be considered a supplement to, not a substitute for, breast milk or formula. Do not attempt to wean your baby completely to solids until he is comfortable and well practiced at drinking from a cup and eating with his fingers or from a spoon.

When you have decided that your child is ready to make the complete transition to solids, simply begin giving him more solids and less liquid from a nipple. Eventually, you should be able to eliminate the breast or bottle from each of your youngster's daily meals. The night-time feeding is frequently the last and most difficult one for a baby to give up. Offering a pacifier or changing the baby's before-bed routine — such as reading a book to him in place of nursing — can sometimes ease the transition.

Begin your baby's transition to solid food with a single-ingredient, iron-fortified baby cereal mixed with breast milk or formula. Rice is particularly recommended as a first cereal because it is nutritious, easy to digest and unlikely to cause any food-intolerance problems. Place a very small amount of the cereal on the tip of a small spoon, then gently slide the spoon and food just inside the baby's lips and let him suck at it. If he spits out the cereal — which is a baby's natural reflexive response at first — try giving it to him again. Gradually, the baby will learn how to move the food to the back of his tongue. You should never try to force swallowing by placing food far back in a baby's mouth. This will only cause the child to gag.

Begin with one or two teaspoons of cereal at each feeding, then gradually increase the amount to four to six tablespoons. After your child is comfortably eating this amount of cereal, you may start to introduce him to other grains, such as oat or barley cereal, as well as gradually adding other solid foods: puréed fruits and vegetables, and puréed or mashed meats.

Always introduce new foods one at a time, and wait a few days after each new item for signs of intolerance, such as excessive spitting up, diarrhea, rash, sore bottom or wheezing. If your child has such a reaction, consult your pediatrician. She may recommend removing these foods from your child's diet until he is several months older. Pediatricians now advise against introducing egg yolks, a traditional starter food, before the baby is nine months of age or so, because the yolks may inhibit the absorption of iron from other foods. Honey, which has been linked to infant botulism, should never be given to babies during the first year.

If your child rejects a particular food, never attempt to make it more palatable by adding salt or sugar. Sugar can lead to tooth decay and too much salt can strain his kidneys. If a food is rejected, try mixing it with a food your child likes, or simply offer another one in its place. Children, like adults, have individual food tastes and preferences that should be respected. Babies and toddlers also seem to have healthy instincts when it comes to nutrition: Studies have shown that if a child is presented with a wide selection of wholesome foods, he will eventually choose enough from among them to receive all the nutrients he needs.

Finger foods By the time a child is seven to nine months old, or has cut several teeth, she will be able to chew and is ready to accept food with coarser

A Schedule for Introducing Solid Food

This chart lists solid foods that doctors recommend introducing in three stages. The texture of the foods becomes increasingly coarse as the child's ability to chew and digest improves. Your child may be ready for a given stage as much as two months before the chart indicates; if you think so, consult his doctor.

Introduce one food at a time, starting with a cereal from the grain group and adding one item from each of the other food groups in turn. Wait three days after offering each new food to watch for any signs of intolerance. Repeat the cycle, adding another new food from each group. Foods within a group are listed in the order they should be introduced — puréed chicken before puréed turkey for a six-month-old, for instance.

The diet is cumulative. Once a food is successfully introduced, make it a frequent feature of the baby's menu, in a coarser form as he gets older. Unless noted otherwise, all the fruits and vegetables listed for the six- and nine-month-olds are cooked.

While commercial baby foods are available, you can prepare foods at home using a grinder *(page 82)* or a food processor. But if you do, you must keep all equipment absolutely clean and use only high-quality ingredients.

Age	Grain products	Meat, fish, poultry	Fruits	Vegetables	Dairy products and gelatin
Six months Smooth, puréed or finely blended; strained commercial baby foods	infant's rice cereal infant's oat cereal infant's barley cereal	chicken turkey veal beef	applesauce pears peaches apricots	carrots squash sweet potatoes peas green beans	none
Nine months Coarse, slightly lumpy or mashed; junior commercial baby foods	oatmeal infant's wheat cereal crackers zwiebacks	lamb liver	raw, ripe bananas raw, ripe pears raw, ripe peaches	white potatoes broccoli zucchini	ice cream cottage cheese pudding egg yolk gelatin

12 months
 Chopped bite-size table foods
	bread
	 rice
		fish
		 hamburger
			seedless orange
			  sections
			 seedless, mashed
			  grapes
				mashed tomatoes
				 mashed legumes
				 peanut butter
				  spread on bread
					whole eggs
					 cheese
					 yogurt

textures, such as cottage cheese, sliced bananas, cooked pasta shells and diced, well-cooked vegetables. Also at this age, a baby is usually eager to attempt eating by herself, either by using her fingers or by dipping a spoon into her food.

Encourage these steps toward independence. Let the child use her fingers to get food to her mouth or give her a spoon to hold and play with while you feed her with another one. Gradually, through trial and error, she will learn how to use the utensil. A small plastic spoon or one with a looped handle specially designed for a baby's small hands should aid the child's learning process.

For safety's sake, some foods should always be kept out of a young child's reach. These include hot dogs, nuts, whole grapes, popcorn and other foods that can cause a baby or toddler to choke. Meats should be carefully diced before being served. Children have also been known to choke on peanut butter, so you should spread it thinly on bread or crackers for easier swallowing.

In choosing table foods, you may also wish to postpone giving your child some of the more common sources of food allergies — corn, fish, onions, citrus fruits, strawberries, cow's milk and egg whites — until she is one year old.

Preparing baby food   Although commercially prepared baby foods are convenient and generally nutritious, many parents opt for the economy of preparing baby foods at home from fresh ingredients. Always wash your hands before preparing baby food and make sure all utensils and work areas are thoroughly cleaned.

Avoid overcooking the food, which can destroy healthful nutrients. Foods for a child who is not yet ready to chew should be carefully puréed and strained to remove all lumps, seeds and skins, which are hard to digest and can cause a baby to choke. For the sake of efficiency, you may wish to prepare the foods in sizable batches using a blender, food processor or baby-food grinder, and then pour the foods into an ice-cube tray and freeze. When frozen, the cubes can be removed and stored in freezer bags. At your child's next meal, you will have a convenient cube-size portion ready to be heated and eaten.

As your baby gets older and begins to eat solids with more assurance and gusto, you may find several items of baby-feeding equipment helpful in keeping messes at a minimum. A high chair equipped with a harness belt can keep a squirming baby stationary during feeding time. Bibs, particularly plastic ones, which can be wiped clean, can save unnecessary laundering. For speed and convenience, you may wish to use bibs that substitute snap-on fasteners for the traditional strings and that have pockets for catching dropped food.

Warming dishes — which are baby-size plates with special hot-water compartments — allow you to keep your baby's food warm throughout an entire meal. Some warming dishes are also equipped with suction cups on the bottom, which prevent the dishes from overturning and making a mess. ∴

Grinding baby food. *To use this grinder, place the food — here, cooked carrots — in the top of the outer cylinder (top). Fit the cutting unit into place and push down the outer cylinder as you crank the device. The solid inner cylinder will force the food up through the cutter and the strainer (bottom).*

About Weaning and Solids

For how long can I safely store an opened jar of baby food in the refrigerator?

You should use a jar of baby food within one to two days of opening it. Never keep jars from which a baby was fed directly. The baby's saliva, transferred by the spoon, will speed the growth of bacteria in the jar.

How should I prepare finger foods for my baby in order to keep her from choking on them?

Crackers and cereals, which break down in the baby's mouth when mixed with saliva, are safe as they are; foods such as cheese, which do not readily break down, should be cut into small, easily digestible pieces. And do not give your child small items such as whole grapes or berries until she can chew.

Will giving my baby solid foods help him sleep through the night?

Though many parents swear by this, there is no scientific proof that solid food is more likely than breast milk or formula to keep a baby content at night.

When I'm spoon-feeding my baby, how can I tell when he's had enough to eat?

He will let you know when he's full by turning his head away, closing his mouth, or pushing the food out with his tongue. When he shows one of these signs two or three times, end the meal.

At what age can my baby begin eating spicy foods?

A child's digestive tract is usually not ready for spicy foods until he is one year old. Even at that age, you should introduce them very slowly.

Can my baby drink diluted tea?

Most teas contain caffeine, a powerful stimulant, and should not be served to children. Water and fruit juices are the best drinks for children.

My baby refuses to eat any kind of

meat. How can I make sure he is getting enough protein?

Babies need a surprisingly small amount of protein — only about one gram per day for each pound of the child's weight. This is equivalent to the protein content of two ounces of breast milk or formula. If a child is eating table foods, then beans, peas and cheese are also excellent sources of protein.

How do I know which of the commercially prepared baby foods are the best for my infant?

Read labels carefully. Make sure that salt, sugar or preservatives have not been added. Also check the expiration date and make sure the center of a jar lid is slightly depressed, indicating that the vacuum seal remains intact.

When I give my baby milk from a cup, should it be whole milk or skim milk?

Children under the age of two should have whole milk rather than low-fat or skim milk. They need the fat in whole milk for energy, to absorb the fat-soluble vitamins, A, D, E and K, and to help their nervous systems develop.

Is it safe to give my baby yogurt?

Yogurt contains all the nutrients of milk, but also may cause the same intolerance problems as milk. For children who like yogurt, it has some added benefits. The benign bacteria cultures in yogurt help the body absorb minerals and manufacture vitamin K. These bacteria also help alleviate constipation, diarrhea and indigestion, and they can prevent harmful organisms, such as those that cause dysentery and salmonella infections, from growing in the intestines. Choose plain or fruit-flavored yogurts that do not contain seeds.

Some foods seem to change the color of my baby's bowel movement. Is this anything to be concerned about?

It is common for beets to turn a baby's bowel movement red and for other vegetables, such as spinach, to turn it green or greenish black. As long as the color change is not accompanied by diarrhea, you should not worry. If diarrhea does occur, omit that food from your child's diet until she is older.

Health and Safety

The first year of life is a vulnerable time for your child, and your natural role is that of guardian and nurse — helping her through illness and protecting her against serious accidents. This section will examine ways of shielding your baby and keeping her healthy. A willing and expert partner in your work will be the child's physician. Through preventive measures such as regular medical checkups, proper immunizations and sound advice on everyday care, the doctor will help lay the groundwork for a healthy, happy life.

But you will retain primary responsibility for your child's well-being. You should be able to recognize the symptoms of illness, know when — and when not — to call for medical attention and learn how to administer medication. Above all, you will want to create a sensibly safe environment for your child. By removing the worst potential physical dangers from the home, you can almost always avoid grievous harm without stifling the child's ingrained curiosity and normal need to explore.

Regular Medical Care

One of the most important decisions you will make as parents is the choice of a doctor for your newborn. The doctor will not only minister to your infant during periods of illness, but will also provide well-baby care. He will offer guidelines for nutrition and hygiene and will suggest ways to stimulate your child's development. He will monitor the baby's growth in every area and will answer any questions about behavior, care or daily routine. Your doctor will be active in your child's health care, so it is essential that you choose someone you trust.

Finding the right physician

Your child's physician can be either a family practitioner who is trained to treat both adults and children — your own doctor, perhaps — or a pediatrician, who specializes in children and adolescents. If you decide to go outside your own sphere of experience, you will probably want to start thinking about a doctor before the baby is born. This will give you ample time to gather recommendations from your obstetrician and local hospital or medical society, and from friends and relatives. Meet with several doctors and take along a list of questions regarding the doctor's practice and his thoughts on child rearing.

Find out first whether the doctor works alone or in practice with others, and who covers for him when he is unavailable. Are there evening and weekend office hours to accommodate working parents? Is the doctor easily reached after hours in case of emergency? And is he affiliated with a good hospital that is convenient to you?

This is also the time to ask about the doctor's views on breast-feeding versus bottle-feeding — or other matters of importance to you and your family. If you have strong feelings on any issues of this sort, discuss them frankly and find out whether the doctor will support you.

During the interview, assess the doctor's personal style. Do you feel at ease talking to him? Does he listen patiently to your concerns and questions and respond in a reassuring manner? Do you feel confident in his ability and approach to child care? Your answers to these questions should all be positive. A first-rate doctor, in fact, would have it no other way, because he, too, is about to embark on a long-term commitment.

The well-baby checkup

The doctor usually examines the newborn in the hospital within 24 hours of birth and sees the baby in his office periodically throughout the first year. The first office checkup usually takes place at two weeks of age; others come at two, four, six, nine and 12 months. At each visit, the doctor will conduct a thorough physical exam. He will evaluate the baby's skin and muscle tone and examine the feet, legs, hips, spine and neck. The baby's weight and length will be recorded, and the circumference of her head will be measured for an indication of brain growth.

The doctor will also check to make sure that the fontanels — the soft spots on the infant's head — are closing correctly. He will listen to the heart and lungs with a stethoscope, inspect the genitalia and palpate the abdomen to check for organ development. The ears, nose, mouth and throat will be examined for development, and the baby's gag reflex checked to be sure he can swallow properly. The doctor will look inside the eyes for obstructions and check the pupils for response to light. He will test hearing by observing the baby's reaction to a sharp noise.

At each visit, the doctor will also look for advances in mental, motor, emotional and social development. He will ask about the child's feeding and sleeping schedules, her temperament and general behavior. Depending on her age, immunizations may also be given *(box, right)*.

A summary of what may occur during each checkup, other than the physical examination, appears below. Keep in mind that the ages specified for completing developmental milestones are rough guidelines only; every child develops at a slightly different rate.

Two weeks
On this visit, the doctor may take a complete family medical history. He may ask for information on the pregnancy and childbirth. He will most likely want to discuss how you are adjusting to life with a new baby.

Two months
The doctor will look for such signs of development as smiling or cooing, grasping an object momentarily and following a moving object briefly with the eyes. At this visit, the infant will be given her first immunizations — an injection to protect against diphtheria, tetanus and pertussis (DTP), and an oral vaccine to guard against polio.

Four months
The doctor will see if the baby tries to grab dangling objects and can hold her head up without support. A second dose of DTP and oral polio vaccines will be administered.

Six months
The doctor will check for emerging teeth; he may recommend that solid foods be added to the baby's diet. Developmental milestones may include reaching for a desired object and the ability to echo spoken sounds. A third injection of DTP vaccine will be given.

Nine months
The doctor will examine the development of the baby's feet and legs, and blood may be tested to check for anemia. He may check to see whether the infant can sit unsupported, crawl or cruise (hold onto things to walk). The baby's new accomplishments may include mastery of the pincer grasp (thumb and forefinger).

12 months
The baby may be walking unsupported and climbing. The doctor will observe the baby's gait for leg or joint problems. The baby may have a spoken vocabulary of one or more words and be able to understand several more in addition. At this time, the child will also be tested to see if she has been exposed to tuberculosis.

The parents' role
At the end of each checkup, your doctor will give you an overall assessment of your baby's health and discuss what to expect in the way of behavioral changes or developmental growth before the next visit. You in turn can prepare for the next appointment by keeping notes on your baby's diet, feeding pattern, sleeping schedule, general behavior and any milestones passed. ⋮

Immunizations in the First Year

To guard against four serious diseases, immunizations begin in the child's first year.

A combined vaccine for diphtheria, tetanus and pertussis (whooping cough), called DTP vaccine, is injected at two, four and six months of age. An oral vaccine against polio is given at two and four months of age.

There are usually no side effects from the polio vaccine. But the area injected with DTP vaccine may redden and swell, and the child may be fussy and develop a slight fever. These symptoms should disappear within 24 hours.

In rare instances, however, the pertussis portion of the DTP vaccine may cause severe side effects. You should call your doctor immediately if your baby develops a fever of 103° F. or higher, appears listless or cries inconsolably for several hours.

Routine Ailments of Infancy

A year will rarely pass during which your youngster does not experience an illness of some sort, and the first 12 months are no exception. Happily, the most frequent ailments are usually not very serious, and they are easily handled in consultation with your child's pediatrician. The all-important first step is learning to recognize the symptoms of illness in an infant.

Early signs of illness

Many parents seem to know instinctively when their child is coming down with an illness. Such intuition, usually based on the slightest change in the child's normal appearance, behavior or routine, can be invaluable as an early warning. Specific symptoms can include skin that is pale or flushed, drowsiness, listlessness, change in appetite and fussing or crying. More seriously, your child may develop a fever of 101° F. or higher taken rectally, diarrhea, change in frequency of urination, difficulty breathing and persistent vomiting that prevents the infant from retaining food and fluids.

Calling the doctor

Any of these strong symptoms warrants a call to the doctor. Before you telephone, however, take a few minutes to organize your thoughts and assemble information.
- Take your baby's temperature *(page 91)* and record the thermometer reading and the time of day.
- Write down any other symptoms, how long they have been present and pertinent details. For example, if diarrhea is present, note how many bowel movements the child has had over a period of time and describe their appearance.
- Have your pharmacy's telephone number close by in case the doctor wants to call in a prescription and keep a pencil and paper handy for writing down the doctor's instructions.

When you call the doctor's office, state your child's full name, age and weight. When the doctor comes on the line, give your report, inform her if any other member of the family is sick and describe that condition.

Illnesses and treatments

In some cases the doctor will ask you to bring the child to her office. Most often, she will prescribe over the phone. Following are the symptoms and treatments of some common childhood ailments. This information is not designed as a substitute for a comprehensive children's medical guide, which every parent should own, nor is it meant to take the place of a consultation with the doctor.

Not included here are acne, cradle cap, colic and diaper rash, which are discussed elsewhere in this volume; check the index for the page numbers.

Eyes

Blocked tear duct. Tears normally drain from the eyes into the nasal passage through a duct at the inside corner of each eye. If the duct has not fully opened or is blocked by mucus, tears overflow and dry to a yellowish white crust that may cake the eyelids together. In some cases the duct becomes infected, causing redness and a discharge of pus. If so, you should telephone your pediatrician, who may suggest a massage technique to open the tear duct or may prescribe medication in case of infection. The dried tears can be wiped away with a moist cloth.

Conjunctivitis. Also called pinkeye, conjunctivitis is an inflammation of the membrane that lines the inner eyelids and covers the whites of the eye. Conjunctivitis, which is usually caused by a viral or bacterial infection, results in redness and swelling around the edges of the eyelids, itching and a puslike discharge — mild if caused by a virus, more severe if caused by bacteria. Viral conjunctivitis should disappear on its own in three days; if not, call the doctor. Conjunctivitis believed to be bacterial should be discussed with a physician, who will likely prescribe an antibiotic ointment or drops.

Ear, nose and throat   *Middle-ear infection.* A middle-ear infection, often a complication of a cold, occurs when one or both of the Eustachian tubes, which drain fluid from the middle ear to the throat, become irritated and swell. Fluid that is trapped in the middle ear becomes infected and builds rapidly, exerting painful pressure on the eardrum. Symptoms of middle-ear infection may include rubbing or pulling at the ears, fever, loss of appetite, crying or irritability. If the eardrum has ruptured under the pressure, there may be a release of pus or a watery discharge. Contact your pediatrician immediately; the usual treatment is a course of antibiotic therapy.

Thrush. Thrush is a yeast infection of the mouth. White patches appear on the tongue and the insides of the cheeks. Thrush is usually not painful and may clear up on its own in time. To speed recovery in severe cases, your doctor may prescribe antifungal drops to coat the affected area.

Croup. Croup is a viral infection of the larynx and the windpipe. The inflammation narrows the child's breathing passages, causing croup's characteristic barking cough and labored breathing. If croup is suspected, call the doctor. To ease the child's breathing, the physician may suggest sitting with the youngster in a closed bathroom filled with steam.

Cold. Colds are viral infections of the upper respiratory passages. Symptoms may include sneezing, nasal congestion, a clear or yellowish nasal discharge, fever, irritability, listlessness, loss of appetite, or cough. In infants under six months, vomiting and mild diarrhea may also be present. Offer the infant plenty of fluids; if nasal congestion makes sucking from breast or bottle difficult, telephone the doctor. She may recommend salt-water nose drops or suctioning mucus from the infant's nose prior to feeding.

Digestive system   *Vomiting.* Babies commonly spit up, or regurgitate, their food, often as a result of overfeeding, feeding too fast or taking in air. True vomiting — the forceful ejection of the stomach's contents — can be a symptom of any number of diseases. After an episode of vomiting, provide only clear fluids for a few hours, then gradually resume milk or formula. But if the child vomits more than twice in two hours, if the vomit contains green bile or if the stomach contents are propelled violently through the air, you should telephone your pediatrician immediately. Also inform the physician if your infant exhibits other signs of illness, such as abdominal pain, high fever, difficulty breathing, headache or drowsiness.

Constipation. Symptoms include a decrease in the number of bowel movements, and hard, dry stools that are difficult for the child to pass. This condition is usually caused by diet — taking in too much milk, for example, or too little fiber or water. But call your doctor before making any dietary changes.

Diarrhea. Diarrhea is characterized by the frequent passage of loose, watery stools. Some common causes of diarrhea are viral infections, overfeeding, an intolerance to a specific food and the taking of antibiotic medicines. Call your doctor, since the fluid loss can cause dehydration quickly in infants, especially if diarrhea is accompanied by vomiting. She will probably recommend a schedule of withholding solid foods, increasing the intake of fluids and then gradually reintroducing solid foods.

Skin *Heat rash.* Heat rash, or prickly heat, occurs when pores are unable to bring sweat to the skin's surface. A bright rash of tiny red pimples appears, usually in skin folds or on the cheeks, neck, chest or diaper area. This condition may appear during hot, humid weather or when a child has a high fever or is too warmly dressed. Give your child a tepid bath and dress him in loose-fitting clothes. If the rash does not improve in a few days, or if blisters appear, you should call the child's pediatrician.

Roseola. Roseola is a viral infection characterized by a high fever of 103° F. to 105° F. that lasts for three to five days. Once the temperature returns to normal, a rash of small red spots develops on the chest, abdomen or back. There is no treatment for roseola, other than to reduce the fever *(box, right)*. Call your doctor if the fever lasts longer than three or four days or if other symptoms such as persistent fussiness or vomiting develop. ❖

The Mystery of Infant Crib Deaths

The ultimate fear of many parents is that their new baby will fall victim to the condition known as sudden infant death syndrome (SIDS) — the unexpected, unexplained death of a presumably healthy infant during sleep. SIDS, sometimes called crib death, takes the lives of about three of every 1,000 babies born each year. The danger of SIDS is greatest between the ages of two and four months; it rarely occurs before two weeks or after six months of age. It seems to strike most frequently in the winter months, and it claims more boy than girl infants. Although little is known about the condition's cause, infants thought to be at high risk are those with a family history of SIDS, infants whose mothers have a history of smoking or who experienced anemia during pregnancy, premature infants, infants with low birth weight and infants who have been diagnosed

as having periods of apnea — a prolonged pause between breaths. Recent research has ruled out earlier theories that SIDS is caused by suffocation due to crib bedding, allergic reactions, bacterial infections or parental negligence.

While doctors are investigating possible links between SIDS and such medical conditions as abnormalities in the central nervous system or an anatomic obstruction of the infant's airway, there is currently no way of preventing SIDS. However, for infants who are at high risk, home monitoring devices are available that sound an alarm to warn parents when dangerous pauses in breathing occur. Parents who use such a device are routinely trained in resuscitation techniques, as well, so that they will be prepared to revive their child. In many cases the sound of the alarm itself startles the child into breathing.

Detecting and Treating a Fever

Often the first sign of illness in a child is fever, yet fever is not actually part of the disease itself. An elevated temperature is, rather, one of the body's infection-fighting agents.

When bacteria or viruses invade the body, chemical messengers respond to the threat by pushing the body's heat-regulating mechanism to a higher level. Internal body temperature then rises, and this excess heat is believed to inhibit the growth and reproduction of the invading infection-causing organisms.

While fever may be beneficial in fighting infection, it must be carefully monitored in babies. This is especially important for infants under the age of four months: Fever may be the only noticeable sign of illness in a young infant, no matter how serious the disease is. Therefore, your doctor may recommend that you call anytime there is a fever present in an infant younger than four months old. For older babies, contact your doctor if the rectal temperature reaches 101° F. or greater. You should also watch for other symptoms of illnesses that commonly cause fever — such as colds, sore throats and earaches — and relay those symptoms to the doctor as well.

To judge if your child has a fever, it helps to know the child's normal temperature. Body temperature fluctuates during the day, with the lowest level occurring in early morning and the highest in early evening. But a baby's rectal temperature generally falls between 97.5° F. and 100° F. Many doctors consider 101° F. to be a low, illness-induced fever.

The rectal method is considered the most accurate means of taking a temperature and is preferred for babies and small children. While more convenient devices for taking temperatures exist, such as heat-sensitive strips that give a reading when pressed to the child's skin or digital-display thermometers that are easy to read, most doctors recommend using the mercury-filled glass thermometer. It is less expensive and more precise than other models, measuring temperatures to within .1° F. of their true reading. The rectal model has a short, round bulb at the working end to facilitate entry into the rectum. Never use an oral thermometer to take a rectal temperature; the slim, pointed tip can damage rectal tissue.

When taking a rectal temperature, hold your child firmly and be prepared to remove the thermometer if he moves suddenly. The preferred method for taking a rectal temperature in a child under six months of age is pictured above. After six months, when the child becomes more active, position him on his stomach across your lap. Place one hand firmly on the

Before taking a rectal temperature, grasp the thermometer by the top of the stem and, with a snapping motion of the wrist, shake it hard until the mercury column falls below 95° F. Then coat the thermometer's bulb with a lubricant, such as petroleum jelly. Lay the baby on his back and lift his heels. Insert the thermometer's tip no more than one inch into the rectum and hold it steady for three minutes. Remove the thermometer, wipe it clean, then rotate it slowly until you see the mercury column appear beneath the numbers; record the number where the mercury column ends. Wash the thermometer with soap and cool water and store it in its case.

youngster's back and with your other hand insert the thermometer and hold it securely in place.

If your child is feverish, the doctor will probably advise against bundling him in too many blankets or clothes, which can trap body heat, and instruct you to give the child plenty of fluids to avoid dehydration. A good rule of thumb is to offer the child something to drink every half hour while he is awake. If your child has been recently weaned from a bottle to a cup, returning him to a bottle just until he is well again can ensure that he takes in the proper amount of fluids.

In cases where the fever is high and the child very uncomfortable, the doctor may recommend acetaminophen, a fever-reducing drug that is available in liquid form. Acetaminophen does not contain aspirin, so it is less irritating to the baby's stomach. Most important, though, acetaminophen does not share aspirin's possible link with the serious and potentially fatal condition, Reye syndrome *(page 92).*

To reduce discomfort, your child's pediatrician may also suggest sponging the child briskly with tepid water for about 20 minutes. This carries heat away from the body as the water evaporates from the skin. You should not give the youngster alcohol or cold-water baths, which can cause shivering and actually lead to an increase in body temperature.

Medicine for Your Baby's Ills

When your baby is ill, the doctor will probably prescribe medicine. Although she or the pharmacist will give you dosage instructions, it is your responsibility to understand the treatment and administer the medication correctly.

Make sure that you know the medicine's name, the form it comes in — liquid, tablet, suppository, ointment — and what it is supposed to do. Ask about side effects or reactions that might occur and how to handle them. If the doctor does not already know, tell her if your baby is allergic to certain medicines. When giving the medication, follow the dosage instructions exactly — how much medication per dose, how often and for what length of time. The instructions will probably appear on the medication's label; if not, write them down before leaving the doctor's office or the pharmacy.

Administering medication properly

There are a number of safeguards to bear in mind when administering medication to children, the most important being always to check the label on the bottle and reread the dosage before giving any medicines. Also, you should never take anything out of the medicine cabinet without proper light; one medicine bottle is easily mistaken for another in dim light.

Most oral medications prescribed for infants come in liquid form and are meted out by the teaspoon — in medical terms, an exact 5 cc of liquid. To make sure you are measuring out the correct amount of medicine, use a calibrated dropper, spoon or syringe, which can be purchased at your drugstore.

Once the child has completed the prescribed course of medication, dispose of any unused portion. Do not save the medicine or give it to another child for the same or a similar illness; the physician has prescribed specifically for this illness in this child, and to administer the medication in a different situation or to a different child could produce a bad reaction. You should also periodically check the expiration dates on the nonprescription items that you keep on hand and throw away any that have expired.

A well-stocked medicine cabinet

In addition to your regular supplies and first-aid kit, you will need certain things specifically for your baby. Two important medications are liquid acetaminophen for reducing fever and relieving pain, and syrup of ipecac, to induce vomiting if your child has swallowed a dangerous substance. You should always check with your doctor or poison-control center, however, before administering ipecac to the child. Some substances will only do more harm to the child's esophagus if brought up by vomiting.

Other items you should stock include antibiotic and diaper-rash ointments, petroleum jelly, a rectal thermometer, a nose dropper, and a calibrated medicine dropper and medicine spoon. You will also want to have a vaporizer, preferably the cool-mist type; it works just as effectively as steam models yet eliminates the possibility of the child's being accidentally burned. ∴

The Threat of Reye Syndrome

Reye syndrome is a dangerous and sometimes fatal condition that in rare cases strikes children recovering from viral infections, usually influenza and chicken pox. The illness affects boys and girls equally and most often strikes youngsters between six and 14 years of age.

Symptoms include persistent vomiting, violent headaches, lethargy and sleepiness. In a short time, the child can lapse into a coma. Call your doctor immediately if these symptoms occur; prompt medical treatment is crucial.

While a specific cause has yet to be determined, evidence seems to link the syndrome to the use of aspirin in a preceding viral illness. You will want to consult your doctor, of course, but a wise alternative might be to substitute the aspirin-free pain reliever acetaminophen in any situation.

Maneuvering Medicines into an Infant

Using a dropper. *Fill a calibrated medicine dropper with the correct amount of liquid. Hold the baby as you would for feeding, with her head in the crook of your arm and her arm secured by your hand. Insert the dropper in the corner of her mouth and position the dropper's tip between the inside of her cheek and her upper gum. Slowly compress the bulb to release the medication.*

Using a medicine spoon. *Pour the correct amount of liquid into the hollow handle of a calibrated medicine spoon, then rest the spoon on a flat surface while you position the baby. Cradle the child as for feeding, holding her free arm in your hand. Place the spoon's edge between her lips and raise it so the medicine runs slowly into her mouth.*

Giving eyedrops. *Lay your baby on her back on a flat surface, having a helper keep the baby's arms still, if possible. Turn the baby's head to one side so that the affected eye is closest to you and gently push down on the cheek skin to expose the channel between the eyeball and lower lid. Steadying your hand on the baby's head, deposit the drops in the channel at the outside corner of the eye.*

Giving eardrops. *Lay your baby on her side, with the infected ear facing up; keep her head still by holding her jaws firmly but gently with one hand and restrain her arms with your forearm. Steady your other hand against the baby's head and deposit the correct number of drops in the ear canal. Keep her head still for about three minutes to ensure thorough coating of the infected area.*

Giving nose drops. *Wipe any excess discharge from the infant's nose, then lay her on her back. With the thumb and fingers of one hand, gently hold the baby's head still and tilted slightly back; restrain her arms with your forearm. Then slowly squeeze the prescribed number of drops into each nostril. Wait a minute, then wipe the baby's nose again or suction to relieve the congestion.*

Inserting a suppository. *Holding the child firmly across your lap with her stomach down, open the buttocks and guide the suppository, tip first, into her rectum with your index finger. When you feel the suppository slide completely in and the rectal sphincter tighten, remove your finger and press the buttocks together for about five minutes.*

Teething and Tooth Care

One of the most memorable events of early childhood is the appearance of that first tooth punctuating a gleeful smile. By the time your baby is a year old, he will probably have six to eight teeth, and by the time he is two to three years of age, a full set of 20 primary, or baby, teeth will have appeared.

Teething miseries

Some babies show no outward signs of teething, while others may be fretful or restless and drool more than usual. The gums usually redden and swell. Most doctors agree that while teething may cause some discomfort, it does not cause fever, runny nose, diarrhea, vomiting or rashes. These are signs of illness, not teething, and warrant a call to the doctor.

Teething misery is usually relieved by chewing on something hard or cold — teething toys or a washcloth wrung out in cold water, for example. Do not freeze water-filled teething toys, however; this practice can cause frostbite. Massaging your baby's gums may ease the pain, but you should consult your doctor before using preparations that numb the child's gums; anesthetics can cause an allergic reaction.

Fighting decay

The teeth and gums should be wiped twice a day with a damp sterile gauze pad to remove plaque, a bacteria-rich film that leads to decay. Limiting both the amount of sugar your baby consumes and the length of time it stays in her mouth reduces the threat of decay. A bedtime bottle of juice or milk leaves small amounts of liquid that pool around the teeth and invite problems. Often called "nursing bottle syndrome," decay from this source may show up on the teeth as white spots, which sometimes turn dark. If your baby must take a bottle to bed, fill it with plain water.

Water itself can be a deterrent to tooth decay if your drinking water contains fluoride, a nutrient that strengthens tooth enamel. If you live in an area with unfluoridated water or if you are nursing your baby, your pediatrician may prescribe supplemental fluoride drops. •ᐟ•

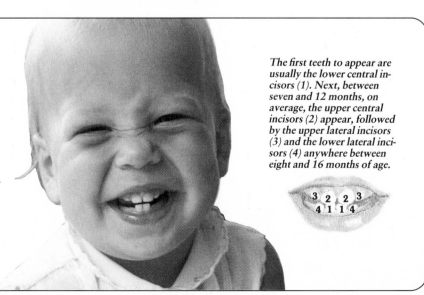

How and When Baby Teeth Appear

A baby's primary teeth begin to form at about the sixth week of pregnancy. At birth, the crown portion of each tooth has developed, the roots are beginning to grow, and even the child's permanent teeth are starting to form.

The first tooth usually breaks through the gums between five and 10 months of age. Typically, this will be one of the lower central incisors, to be followed closely by the other lower central incisor. Although the age at which teeth erupt may vary slightly for each child, the order of arrival is generally the same, as shown in the diagram at right.

The first teeth to appear are usually the lower central incisors (1). Next, between seven and 12 months, on average, the upper central incisors (2) appear, followed by the upper lateral incisors (3) and the lower lateral incisors (4) anywhere between eight and 16 months of age.

Childproofing Your Home

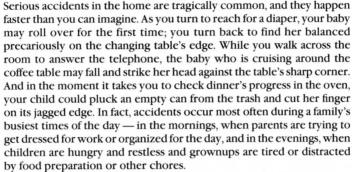

Doorknob guard. *To prevent youngsters from opening doors, a guard like the one shown above can be slipped over the doorknob. The knob only turns if rubber grommets on the guard's sides are squeezed hard enough to grip the doorknob.*

Cabinet lock. *To lock adjoining cabinet doors, one bar of this device is slipped under the handles; a lock pushed into place grips the teeth on the bar. A button on the lock releases the grip, and the lock slides off.*

Outlet caps. *These plastic safety caps fit tightly into unused electrical outlets. Only by inserting a fingernail into a tiny slot at the top of the cap and pulling outward can you remove it.*

Serious accidents in the home are tragically common, and they happen faster than you can imagine. As you turn to reach for a diaper, your baby may roll over for the first time; you turn back to find her balanced precariously on the changing table's edge. While you walk across the room to answer the telephone, the baby who is cruising around the coffee table may fall and strike her head against the table's sharp corner. And in the moment it takes you to check dinner's progress in the oven, your child could pluck an empty can from the trash and cut her finger on its jagged edge. In fact, accidents occur most often during a family's busiest times of the day — in the mornings, when parents are trying to get dressed for work or organized for the day, and in the evenings, when children are hungry and restless and grownups are tired or distracted by food preparation or other chores.

You can help protect your child from serious accidents by becoming aware of potential dangers in your home and correcting them. The surest way to accomplish this is to put yourself on the child's level — literally, if necessary. Observed from the vantage point of a baby who has just started crawling, the mysterious holes of an empty electrical outlet seem just the place to poke curious fingers. And for a child pulling herself up to a wobbly stand, the stem of a pole lamp is just the right size to grasp. By trying to see everything through your little one's adventurous eyes, you should be able to pinpoint potential dangers in every room of your house. Then, to make a good start toward childproofing your home, use the safety devices shown on this page to lock cabinets and doors, cap electrical outlets, pad sharp table edges and block stairways. More suggestions for assessing your home and making it a safer place for your baby appear on pages 96-97.

Another important step is to be prepared in case an accident does occur. Major emergencies require swift professional attention, but since most minor mishaps can be treated at home, you should invest in a good first-aid book and maintain a well-stocked first-aid kit.

It is also a good idea to enroll in a comprehensive first-aid course — one that covers methods of treating cuts, burns, bruises and profuse bleeding, as well as the proper handling of choking or accidental poisoning episodes. More advanced courses may include instruction in cardiopulmonary resuscitation (CPR) — the technique for restarting the heart and breathing if they have stopped. Check with your local hospital or American Red Cross chapter for information on where you can attend such classes. For immediate reference in case of any illness or emergency, keep your doctor's phone number and that of the local poison-control center at your fingertips. You may wish to tape the numbers to each phone in the house. And if you leave your child in someone else's care, be certain that person knows where to reach you, or if you will be unreachable, how you want to have an emergency handled.

Corner guards. *Soft rubber guards like these can cushion falls into sharp table corners. Most guards come with an adhesive tape that will not mar the furniture's finish when the guard is removed.*

Cabinet latch. *This latch has two parts: A catch screws into the doorframe, and a latch with a hooked end screws inside the door. When the door is opened, the hook and catch interlock; pressing down on the latch releases the lock.*

Safety gate. *The safety gate pictured below has two sliding sections that adjust the width and are held in place by a tension bar. Other models fasten to the doorframe by screws and hinges.*

Keeping Your Baby Out of Harm's Way

The old adage that children are accidents waiting to happen has a grain of truth to it. Each year, in addition to the countless number of babies who receive bumps and bruises in minor mishaps, nearly a thousand infants die as a result of accidents on the road and at home. Most accidents in the home, of course, are not really the fault of small children, who are merely following their natural curiosity, but of an environment that is arranged with only adults in mind.

To safeguard your baby against potential dangers in and around the home, think ahead to his next stages of development. If he will be crawling or walking in a month or so, look at things from a child's-eye view and eliminate hazards he might encounter in the areas listed below. Such foresight will not forestall every bump or bruise, but it will certainly help you to prevent the serious accidents and emergency situations that can arise in the nicest of homes.

Accidents in cars
- Always place your child in a car seat and securely buckle the safety straps.
- Lock the car doors when you are inside; an older baby who can reach the door handles may be able to open them.
- Never leave your child unattended in a car.

Burns
- Do not smoke when caring for your baby. Keep cigarettes, matches and lighters out of reach.
- Do not carry hot food or a hot drink while holding your baby; he may grab for it quickly and unexpectedly.
- Place screens in front of stoves, fireplaces and heaters.
- In the kitchen, keep the handles of pots and pans turned toward the back of the stove. To avoid splatters from frying foods or boiling liquids, use the back burners only.
- Keep the baby's high chair away from the stove.
- At the dinner table, avoid passing hot dishes over the baby's head; keep plates and place mats beyond his reach.
- Before a bath, test the temperature of the water in the tub with your elbow or the inside of your wrist; set your hot-water heater no higher than 125° F.

Choking
- Toys should not have small ends that could lodge in a child's mouth; the largest rattle known to have choked a child had ends one and five eighths inches in diameter.
- Check the floors daily for small objects that a crawling baby could put in his mouth and swallow.

- Do not feed your baby small, hard bits of food such as raw carrots, popcorn or nuts. Store these foods and others, such as dried beans, out of the baby's reach.

Cuts
- If a glass or dish shatters on the floor, vacuum the area thoroughly to be sure all slivers are removed.
- Dispose of all empty cans promptly; the sharp edges around the can's edge can easily slice through a baby's skin.
- Keep trash cans out of the baby's reach.

Drowning
- Never leave a small child unattended in the bathroom or bathtub; unplug the telephone so you are not tempted to leave, even briefly, if it rings.
- Place a rubber mat or nonskid treads in the bathtub.
- Always keep the lid of the toilet bowl closed; small children can fall in head first and drown.
- Never leave your child unattended in a wading pool.
- Cover any garden or swimming pools with nylon net when not in use; fence in swimming pools and keep the gate locked.

Electric shock
- Block unused electrical outlets with safety covers.
- Unplug appliances and lamps when not in use and coil their cords out of reach. Fasten electrical cords to walls to prevent the baby from pulling or chewing on them.
- Be sure not to place your baby's playpen near electrical outlets or heaters.
- Put bulbs in empty sockets.
- Do not leave hair dryers or any other electrical appliances plugged in in the bathroom; they could electrocute the baby if they fall into the tub.

Falls
- Never leave your baby unattended on changing tables, beds, sofas or chairs or in walkers.
- Always fasten the safety belt around your child when he is in the high chair.
- Anchor rugs and carpets in place; avoid slippery floors by keeping wax to a minimum.
- Install safety gates at the top and bottom of stairways. Use a gate with a straight top and rigid mesh or vertical slats spaced not more than four and one quarter inches apart *(page 95)*; the baby's head can get stuck in the large

V- or diamond-shaped openings of an accordion-type gate.
- Always keep the sides of the baby's crib raised and locked. As the baby grows, lower the level of the mattress.
- Do not place the crib under a window; a child can push against a screen and fall out. Open windows from the top instead of the bottom, if possible.

Furniture dangers

- Pad the sharp corners of tables that are the baby's height. A baby pulling himself up or learning to walk is unsteady on his feet and may seriously injure himself by falling into a sharp corner.
- Remove tablecloths from the reach of a child pulling up or learning to walk.
- Remove or anchor objects such as pole lamps that a baby may grab and pull over onto himself.
- Use a toy box without a lid or one with supports that hold the lid up in any position.

Garage, basement and storeroom perils

- Keep doors to these areas locked.
- Store all dangerous substances, such as paints, solvents, insecticides, fertilizers and laundry soaps, out of reach.
- Place all tools where a child cannot reach them; disconnect power tools that are not being used.

Medications

- Keep all medicines in a locked cabinet; ask your pharmacist for childproof safety caps.
- Do not tell a child that medicine tastes like candy; this will encourage him to swallow any medicine within reach.
- Instruct houseguests to store medications on a high shelf, not bedside tables or other accessible places.
- Ask guests to place purses and briefcases out of a

child's reach, since they often contain medicines.
- Dispose of old medications by flushing them down the toilet, not by throwing them in the trash.

Outdoor hazards

- Be aware of poisonous plant leaves, nuts or berries your child may put in his mouth.
- Be cautious when using barbecues; set up a screen around the barbecue to keep an exploring child away.

Poisons

- Know which houseplants are poisonous and remove them from your home; a baby will put anything into his mouth, and plant leaves are no exception.
- Use safety locks on all cabinets containing household cleaners, bleaches, polishes and waxes.
- If the telephone or doorbell rings while you are working with a dangerous substance, take it with you to the telephone or door.
- Store pet foods and edible substances that are potentially toxic when swallowed in large quantities, such as food extracts and vitamin tablets, out of a child's reach.
- Place all toiletries, including cosmetics and hair-care products, on a high shelf.

Sharp objects

- Keep knives, scissors, razors and other sharp objects out of a child's reach.
- When changing diapers, keep diaper pins out of reach.

Strangulation

- Move your baby's playpen or crib well away from any drapery or window-shade cords; the baby could become entangled in the cords and strangle.
- Never use elastic to stretch a toy across the crib; make sure crib toys do not have strings longer than 12 inches.

Suffocation

- Always keep the sides of a playpen in the upright position; when folded down, the sides create pockets in which a child could suffocate.
- Do not place pillows in an infant's crib; they can interfere with breathing.
- Dispose of plastic bags immediately after you have emptied them; a youngster can suffocate if he puts a plastic bag over his head.

A Year of Remarkable Development

For your baby, the first 12 months on earth are truly revolutionary, a time of unparalleled physical growth and behavioral change. In one short year she triples her birth weight and develops from a person who is asleep most of the time into one who spends most of her hours awake. Her bodily functions evolve from disorganized and wholly unpredictable states to relatively regular routines. She changes her posture from purely horizontal to a number of stances that enable her to crawl, stand and perhaps even take a few steps. Her muscles, weak and uncontrolled at birth, work into well-toned instruments of physical activity, making her, pound for pound, nearly as strong as an adult weight lifter.

Most significant of all, your baby is developing a mind and personality of her own during these 12 months. She discovers how to influence people and manipulate objects for her own ends. She learns how to communicate in an organized way, if not yet through understandable speech, then at least in sounds, syllables and perhaps a few words that will flower into coherent talk soon enough. She becomes adept with her sensory equipment, associating sounds and sights, tastes and smells, and develops marked preferences. And she lays the foundations of her memory, storing a steady stream of experiences that will guide her actions as new situations and challenges present themselves in the years to come.

No two babies develop at the same rate or with the same degree of comfort. But as the pages that follow will show, generalized sequences of growth — in physical activity, in sensory awareness, and in emotional and social development — include a succession of notable milestones. Those milestone developments tend to occur at fairly predictable times, give or take a couple of weeks in the early part of the first year and a couple of months at the end. By applying these development guidelines loosely, parents can become attuned to their child's maturing process and respond accordingly.

Forces That Shape the Pace of Learning

Babies are born programed to learn and eager to start. The pace of a baby's development is determined by his personality, the maturity of his muscle and nervous systems and the environment created by his parents. Parents provide the practical learning opportunities, the stimulation and the emotional encouragement that make it possible for the baby to develop to the full extent of his potential.

Your baby's personality

A baby's personality and temperament have a lot of effect on when and how comfortably he passes each developmental milestone. For decades, scientists were convinced that the environment provided by the parents — that is to say, nurture rather than nature — determined a baby's personality. Parents had only to perfect their child-rearing techniques to turn difficult babies into easy ones. But modern studies reveal that babies are born with a basic personality package shaped by genetic inheritance and by experiences in the womb and during the birthing process. Parental practice can, in time, modify these inborn traits — negatively as well as positively: A happy baby who is ignored and unloved will become a sad baby. But for at least the first several months of life, the temperament the child is born with controls his behavior.

To assess an infant's personality, researchers look at several areas of behavior, from sleeping and eating to playing and cuddling. A baby's activity level is the most easily identifiable area. Some babies move their arms and legs a great deal when awake, are reluctant to stop sucking at the end of feeding and thrash about during sleep. Other babies move very little, even when they are awake and alert. While there is no totally predictable relationship between the newborn's activity level and muscle development, the more active baby probably will reach muscle-control milestones sooner than the less active youngster. But this same high-activity child may experience an associated delay in areas of sensory or social development.

Regularity of feeding and digestion is another factor. Some babies function smoothly almost from the beginning; others have unruly systems that are in flux for months. Obviously, the untroubled baby is likely to have more of his energies available for physical and social development than the baby who is distracted by digestive discomforts. Babies show distinct differences in their adaptability, too, be it to food, people, places, activities or toys: Some approach the unfamiliar eagerly, others withdraw. The adaptable child is liable to slide into new undertakings without a fuss, while the more cautious child may move one step forward and two steps back, taking longer to claim each new skill but learning it just as well in the end.

Differences appear in babies' sensory thresholds, too. Some are much more aware than others of changes in light, sound and touch, and respond more strenuously to those changes. His own high awareness and vigorous responses can overstimulate such an infant: He will tire sooner and absorb new information more slowly than a calmer baby.

Persistence in the face of frustration is still another part of the child's personality that has a strong bearing on development. One child will discover the grasping ability of his hands by sheer repetition of certain muscle movements day after day. Another, finding no immediate success, will lose interest in grasping after one try, even becoming angry when a parent tries to reengage him. For the easily discouraged child, mastery of a new skill may have to wait for weeks.

Basic personality types

Recognizing your baby's personality type and adjusting the stimulation you give will help you coax him along at his own natural pace of development. Most babies fall midway between the extremes of temperament. If your child fits this middle-of-the-road description, he is generally referred to as an "easy," or average, baby. Such babies are usually in a good mood and adjust quickly to new situations. These children will reach most of their developmental milestones at about the times predicted in the charts that follow in this section.

If, on the other hand, your baby is highly active and easily distracted, he fits within the personality category of the "difficult," or active, infant; one who is often hard to handle. He may well settle into a calmer mood in a few months, after he has devised a way of slowing himself down when he feels overstimulated — by sucking his hand or thumb, for example. Meanwhile, his development may be erratic, surging ahead in one area, falling behind temporarily in another.

Or yours may be a "slow to warm up" baby, one who is generally withdrawn, who inexplicably alternates between smiling and fussing, who rejects anything new. These children perhaps present the most developmental problems and need more than average attention in the early months. The parent of such a child has to learn to walk the narrow line between patient coaxing and impatient pushing, introducing new stimulation at a pace carefully geared to the child's ability to cope.

How a baby learns

Your baby's big job in this first year is to discover himself and his physical capabilities. Fortunately, he is born with an insatiable desire to do just that. His first tools for learning are his senses: sight, hearing, smell, touch and taste. Most of these are already in a near-mature stage of development when the infant is born, vision being the most notable exception; a newborn sees blurred images, even at close range.

The growing memory of an infant is another tool; memory makes it possible for him to associate certain events with predictable consequences. The baby whose infant chair happens to be frequently positioned near the refrigerator gradually learns that the closing of the door makes a sound. When he has incorporated this piece of information, he will anticipate the noise by showing signs of being startled a split second before the door shuts.

Your baby develops his voluntary muscle coordination somewhat more slowly, showing the earliest progress in the head and neck area and moving by stages downward through the body and out to its extremities; control of legs and feet comes last. Development of muscle control depends in the first instance on the growth of nerve-cell connections, both in the brain and elsewhere throughout the nervous system. But if that growth is progressing normally, the baby will employ a combination of imitative behavior, trial and error, and memory to gain control of his muscles. He first masters his facial muscles (a purposeful, social smile will tell you he has achieved this), then his neck muscles, his trunk, arms, hands, legs and feet, until finally he is ready to crawl. Imitative behavior and an increasing ability to differentiate among sounds will put him on the path to talking. Trial and error keep him moving toward goals such as the ability to grasp something. When the first try proves unsuccessful, the baby who has reached the appropriate stage of development will change his technique slightly and try again. Both the early errors and the final success have learning value.

The parents' role   As a parent, you provide several key ingredients in your infant's healthy development: verbal and social stimulation, a rich and interesting environment, and consistent encouragement and love that keep the naturally motivated child learning and exploring. One of the most important things you can do is to talk often and warmly to your infant from the start. Though your baby will not at first understand the words you say, he is receiving information. Filmed studies reveal that even in the first month of life, infants can synchronize their body movements to the speech rhythms of their parents, a fact that suggests a baby may learn the wonders of speech with his whole body.

So make your child's surroundings interesting to all his senses. Give him a variety of things to touch and handle, things to intrigue him visually through their movement, color, shape and pattern, things that produce pleasant sounds and noises. And give him plenty of affectionate attention. Do not worry about spoiling him. Your support at this stage teaches him that there are people who love him and whom he can trust, and these notions build his confidence and enhance his potential for learning. Parental attention comes in many forms — in cuddling, in keeping him where family activities are going on so he can watch and listen, and most especially in play. Rattles, balls and gradually more sophisticated toys have a useful role as your child matures, but games with Mom and Dad are the best form of play now and for years to come.

During games — as in talking, cuddling or any other form of interaction with your child — stay alert for cues that the baby gives you. If he turns his head aside when you have been making eye contact and talking to him, he may be letting you know he is ready to quit and rest for a while. If he smiles and waves his arms when you approach, he may be signaling that he is ready to start a game. No interchange is so valuable a learning experience as the one your baby himself initiates.

If your child has an easy personality, your relationship will probably get off to a smooth start and stay that way. But if your baby is difficult or slow to warm up, remember that this is simply the way he is. Try not to think that his difficulties are somehow your fault. Once you get to know his quirks and special needs, you both will relate to each other more comfortably, and by his first birthday you may realize that he has become an easier child after all. ∴

Charting the Changes That 12 Months Bring

On the pages that follow, a baby's first year is divided into six developmental periods of varying lengths. For each period, the key milestones in four different categories of development are described in detail. The categories are muscle control and body awareness, hearing and language, vision and perception, and emotional and social development.

These charts can be a guide to what to expect from your baby as she progresses, but beware of regarding them as rigid timetables. Babies develop in fairly predictable patterns, but at different rates. The rates are seldom indicators of intelligence or health. Because individual personality and the maturity of the child's neurological system determine how quickly a baby can move from one milestone to the next, variations in the timing of these developments are not unusual.

Parents are sometimes tempted to try to hurry their baby's intellectual and physical growth, introducing particular activities and toys before the child shows signs of readiness for them, in the hope that with coaching she will become proficient earlier than she would otherwise. But child psychologists caution that too much pressure can lead to frustration, loss of self-confidence and resentment. Learning is best achieved when the learner feels joy in her own effort and approval from those close to her. And quite apart from how a baby feels about it, impatient pushing simply does not work.

If your child is developmentally ready to learn a new skill, however, you can provide the opportunity and the stimulus that will cause her to attempt it. You can offer your baby the materials, the challenge and your loving encouragement without being guilty of pushing her. Parents have been interacting with children in this way — helping them learn, sometimes without realizing it — since the dawn of civilization.

For this reason, the chart for each of the six periods is followed by descriptions of games and learning activities that you can try when your baby is at a particular stage of development. These are grouped into the same four development categories, although any one of the activities may actually stimulate your child's progress in two or more areas at once. You may already know most of them, since many are old favorites that your parents probably used with you. In that case, at least you will now be informed about just how a particular game encourages your child's development — and can take whatever satisfaction you may find in knowing that it and all the other activities in this section are recommended by child development authorities. At the end of each list is a brief description of toys that the experts consider especially valuable for that age group.

These photographs represent six major developmental milestones in a baby's first year of life. Left to right and descending: a newborn child turns her head from side to side; a three-month-old boy smiles to the thrill of soaring; a girl in her sixth month sits erect; a seven-month-old crawls; a nine-month-old stands holding onto a chair; and an 11-month-old almost-toddler tests her balance.

103

The First Month

month	1	2	3	4	5	6	7	8	9	10	11	12

The first 30 days in the life of your newborn can be compared to a runner's warm-up. It is a time for her to get organized — to test and limber up her muscles, brain, and other major organs and systems — before setting out on the fast-paced marathon of development that lies ahead. Right now, the newborn's amazing competency derives in part from a set of reflexive behaviors that require no experience, no associations, no understanding on her part to function *(pages 18-19)*. In this month you will observe her trying out a new set of behaviors that are voluntary rather than reflexive. You can see it in the more deliberate way she moves her arms, legs and head, and in her increased responsiveness to sensory stimulation. These are important signs that your baby is getting actively involved in her world.

Muscle Control and Body Awareness

During this first month a baby's muscle control improves noticeably. The jerkiness of her movements in the early weeks gives way to vigorous flexing of the arms and legs in a smoother fashion. Even more impressive, she learns how to push an object away from her face if she feels threatened. Her neck muscles may develop the strength to enable her to raise her head just enough to turn it when she is lying prone. And her clenched hands and flexed legs and feet are beginning to relax.

Hearing and Language

A baby begins to associate the things she hears with things she sees and feels, showing a preference for some sounds. Possibly because of her womb experience, she usually finds higher, female voices more soothing than the low pitch of a male voice. Interestingly, men seem to understand this instinctively, speaking in a higher than normal tone and softening their voices whenever they address a newborn. Toward the end of this month, you may begin to hear nuances of meaning in what has been your baby's all-purpose wail, slight differentiations that tell you whether she is crying because she is hungry, tired or in pain. And she begins to make small, throaty noncrying sounds.

Vision and Perception

By the time she is a month old, your infant probably will be interested in all the activities and objects that can be brought into her visual focal range — but that range is still limited to between eight and 18 inches. By now her eyes are coordinated most of the time. Although she still has relatively little head movement, she eagerly follows a moving object with her eyes. She may show particular pleasure in a simple mobile that hangs to the side of her crib, which is easier to see and safer than a mobile hung overhead. She also likes the contrast of light and dark patterns more than vividness of color. No pattern is more interesting to her, however, than the human face with its lively features. Babies study all faces that enter their vision; they especially like watching changing expressions of familiar faces.

Emotional and Social

By the end of the first month, a baby has likes and dislikes that perceptive parents will recognize and respond to, to their child's gratification. In return, she begins to feel positive emotions toward people. Most especially, she begins to forge bonds of love with the person who is her primary caregiver, usually her mother. Simply being picked up and cuddled by this person may be enough to reassure her when she is unhappy. The child learns to adjust her body posture to that of the person holding her, sometimes grasping a part of the holder's body as if returning the hug. Toward the end of the first month, she may give her parents a wonderful gift: her first real smile.

This mother smiles because she hopes her smile will comfort her crying month-old baby. Crying is the infant's primary means of communication — employed to signal hunger, a cold wet diaper, the discomfort of a gas bubble that needs to be burped up or simple fatigue.

The baby turns her head from side to side to track the movement of a soft bunny in her mother's hand. Such simple activities provide the young child with both mental and physical exercise.

The mother and infant at right are engaged in a complex but quite common interaction that promotes bonding. The baby gazes intently at her mother for a few seconds, then looks away. The mother will wait patiently for the baby to reestablish eye contact. This pattern continues for three to five minutes before the baby tires.

A baby discovers calming comfort in sucking on her fist. As she becomes more adept, she may begin sucking on her thumb or individual fingers.

At one month of age, the baby above is able to turn her head from side to side while lying on her stomach. But she can lift her head only high enough for her chin to clear the mattress, and the whole process is done in stages rather than as a fluid motion. It may take 30 seconds or more to complete.

Activities and Games

Muscle Control and Body Awareness

Baby massage In the first weeks of life, your newborn gradually begins to discover her own body and to learn how to move parts of it voluntarily. You can aid her body awareness by gentle massage. Start by rubbing her arms or legs with the flattened palm of your hand, working toward the center of her body.

Rhythm and movement While your baby lies on her back, sing to her and move her arms up and down to the rhythm of the song. In the same manner,

grasp her feet and gently move her legs in a bicycling motion. These exercises not only tone muscles but encourage a consciousness of rhythm. Two to five minutes is long enough for one of these sessions; watch your baby closely. If she seems unhappy or averts her eyes, it is probably because she is tired of the activity, and you should stop.

New textures You can enlarge your baby's experience of textures by stroking her hands and arms with fabric — silk, velvet, flannel, terry cloth, wool. Watch carefully to be sure your child is enjoying this. Some babies are made uncomfortable by a light, ticklish touch.

Hand practice Stimulate your baby's grasp by touching the palm of her hand with your finger. At this time, the resulting grasp is purely reflexive and short-lived, but the exercise strengthens her finger muscles and sets the stage for controlled grasping, which will be one of the child's first voluntary and sustainable muscle skills. You can make the activity fun for both of you by talking to your infant as you gently shake the grasping hand.

Hearing and Language

Making music When you sing nursery rhymes to your baby, softly clap your hands to emphasize the song's cadence. Enliven her spirits by playing a radio, record player or music box near her crib, but do so only when the child is alert, not when she is drifting off to sleep. And do not leave the sound on as background music: You want your baby to learn to attend to sounds, not ignore them.

Naming Hold the baby in your arms or sit on the floor and prop her against your raised knees. As you make eye contact with her, say her name so that she can begin to recognize the sound. Also call her name whenever you approach the crib to pick her up.

Where is the sound coming from? Lay your baby on her back on the floor. Kneel behind her head and hold a rattle about a foot above her. Shake the rattle until her eyes find it. Slowly move the toy from side to side as your child pursues it with her eyes. You can use your voice for a similar purpose. Stand behind the head of the baby's crib where she does not see you. Speak to her, then lean into her field of vision as you continue speaking, so she will make the connection between your voice and your presence.

Vision and Perception

Changing perspectives Vary the baby's view by occasionally moving her crib to different parts of the room. Change her position in the crib for her waking periods, shifting her from back to stomach, and from the head of the crib to the foot.

Visual delight Faces are a favorite with newborns. Prop a picture with bold, contrasting colors, like this one of the smiling sun, against one side of the crib for a while. Then move it to the other side so your baby is drawn to turn her head. Remove the picture from the crib when you

leave. A special infant safety mirror fixed to the side of the crib can give her even more visual excitement as she looks at herself.

Silly games Bring your face close to the baby's. Let her follow your face with her eyes as you move from side to side. Make buzzing and smacking noises. Flutter your eyelids while you hold her fingers just within touching distance so she can watch and feel at the same time. For a sensory surprise, blow gently onto her face.

Light show In a dimly lit room, move the beam of a flashlight back and forth in front of your baby — but never into her eyes. See if she tracks its motion. All such visual tracking exercises give practice in following moving objects.

Emotional and Social

Making conversation Talk to your baby frequently: not in baby talk but in real sentences, properly enunciated. She is not ready to understand you in the conventional sense, but she can pick up your mood from the tone of your voice and will begin to understand that communication is good, that people who love one another show it in this way as in many others. For the same reason, try reading aloud to your baby — not only children's books but even the daily paper or any book you are reading. At her age, the material does not matter, but the sound of your voice is delightful.

Kissing and cuddling Cuddle your baby often. Touch her whenever you feel the instinct. Pick her up when she cries and try to offer her the comfort she is telling you she needs. Rock her. Hold her close. Smile at her and kiss her frequently. By giving her plenty of security and reassurance at this time, you are helping her to develop into a confident, competent and loving child.

The mobile infant Carry your baby with you in an infant sling when you move about the house, shop or go out for a stroll — indeed, anywhere that you feel comfortable with her and where she can travel in reasonable safety. For family mealtimes, place the baby in her infant seat where she can be a part of the activities — on the table itself, if need be.

The Toy Box

The best toys for a baby's first month are people, especially her parents. But the following items can help you stimulate interaction with your baby: a safe, sturdy rattle that is too large to swallow; a soft mobile of stuffed fabric; a music box; and an infant-safe mirror attached securely inside the crib.

Months Two, Three and Four

month	1	2	3	4	5	6	7	8	9	10	11	12

You will observe frequent signs of your baby's emerging self-will in his activities during the second through fourth months. As his reflexive behavior gradually recedes, he increasingly takes charge of his own body and actions. Continually probing with his eyes, mouth and hands, he discovers where his body ends and the rest of the world begins. The baby is delighted to find that his actions, such as shaking or striking a noise-making toy, can make things happen in his physical surroundings.

At the same time, the baby develops a repertoire of sounds, from cooing to babbling, that enables him to express his wants with less crying. As his endearing smile brings a warm and obliging response from adults, giving him a measure of control over them, he smiles more and more often. He recognizes members of his family and becomes more attached to individuals, especially his mother.

Muscle Control and Body Awareness

Straightening his body little by little from the curled posture of life in the womb, the two-month-old arches his back, throws out his arms and legs, stretches his fingers and toes, and twists from side to side. A month later, the baby can lie on his tummy with his pelvis flat, legs extended.

The pleasure he gets from increased control of his body spurs him to constant physical activity. He circles his arms above his head and bicycles his legs in smooth, rhythmic mo-

tions. While on his tummy, he may rock like an airplane, arms and legs out, back arched. You must watch your infant closely when he is on a table or a bed to make sure that he does not fall off as he wriggles around and eventually rolls over from his stomach to his back.

Your baby studies his hands and gradually learns that he can open and close them, bring them together, move them around at will, and stretch and wiggle his fingers. If you place a toy in his hand, he may hold it a few moments, then let it go. If a toy is held in front of him, he will reach toward it with both hands, although he may not be able to grasp it. Later he will swipe at the dangling toy with increasing accuracy, eventually closing on it. In his fourth month, he probably will be able to grasp it with either hand and bring it to his mouth.

As a baby gains more control over his neck muscles, he enjoys shifting his head position for new views of his environment. Early in this period, when propped up for sitting, he can hold his head erect for only a few seconds, but the time lengthens as he grows older and stronger. At two months of age, when lying on his stomach, the child can lift his head to an angle of about 45 degrees. A month later, he is pushing himself up with his arms so that his chest is raised from the mattress and his head is vertical as he inspects the world about him.

By the end of the fourth month, the baby's trunk has greatly strengthened. With pillows or an infant seat for support, the child can sit up for longer and longer periods. When lying on his back, the baby can press his chin to his chest to study his feet or lean his head far back to see what is beyond the normal upward limit of his field of vision.

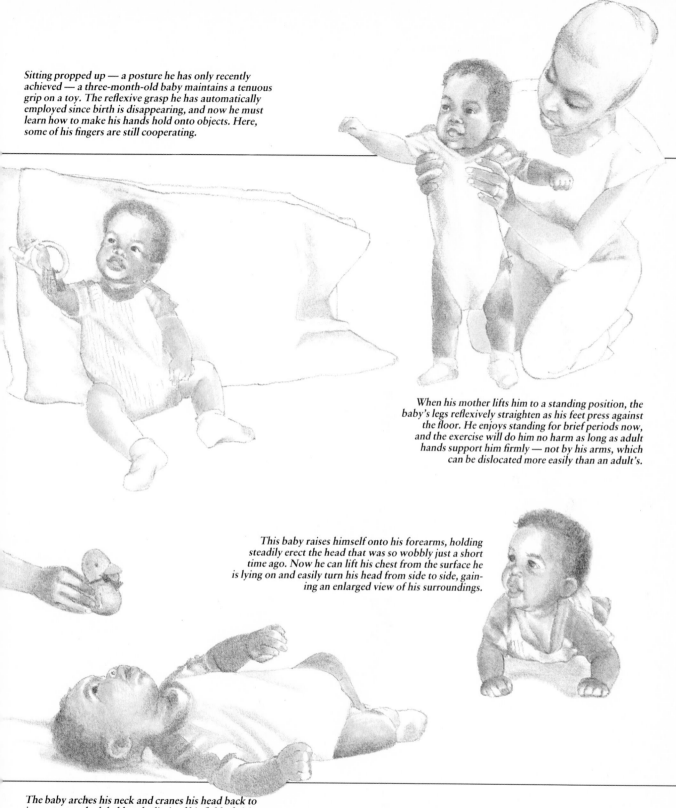

Sitting propped up — a posture he has only recently achieved — a three-month-old baby maintains a tenuous grip on a toy. The reflexive grasp he has automatically employed since birth is disappearing, and now he must learn how to make his hands hold onto objects. Here, some of his fingers are still cooperating.

When his mother lifts him to a standing position, the baby's legs reflexively straighten as his feet press against the floor. He enjoys standing for brief periods now, and the exercise will do him no harm as long as adult hands support him firmly — not by his arms, which can be dislocated more easily than an adult's.

This baby raises himself onto his forearms, holding steadily erect the head that was so wobbly just a short time ago. Now he can lift his chest from the surface he is lying on and easily turn his head from side to side, gaining an enlarged view of his surroundings.

The baby arches his neck and cranes his head back to inspect a toy duck held at the limit of his field of vision. Wide eyes and open mouth indicate the intensity of his concentration, but his hands remain near his sides. He has developed head control faster than limb control and would have difficulty reaching from this position.

Hearing and Language

Becoming more attentive to sounds, babies can now routinely locate the source of a noise with their eyes and can differentiate footsteps from voices. By the time a baby is two months old, he can pick out his mother's voice from a group of others in conversation. Now when you speak to him, he listens intently, watching your eyes and mouth. Babies sometimes even stop sucking at breast or bottle just to listen more attentively.

His verbal skills improve, too, as he progresses from differentiated cries to sounds that are closer to speech: whimpers, cooing sounds, gurgling noises and squeals. As he hears you speak, he seems to begin to understand that messages are made up of syllables and starts uttering vowel sounds of one syllable, such as "aah" and "ooh."

Before long, he is stringing together a series of syllables when talking to you and sometimes for his own amusement when he lies alone in his crib.

Vision and Perception

At the beginning of this period, a baby's visual focus is still limited to objects eight to 18 inches away. But over the next three months, he will be able to see as well as an adult, the lenses of his eyes adjusting to a variety of focal lengths so that he can perceive distance and depth.

Earlier, the baby had difficulty fixing both eyes on an image; his binocular vision was still unsteady. But by the end of this phase, he can even lock his gaze onto moving objects several feet away from him. And now the baby can see in full color, although he prefers two primary hues: blue and red.

He will study a plastic rattle ring placed in his hand and wave it about, enjoying the movement and the noise he is creating. He will be especially pleased if the ring is boldly colored, which he prefers to pastel hues. Interested in details now, he studies the ring's size, shape, the patterns and the play of light on it. If he drops the ring, he will stare, puzzled, at the place from which it disappeared.

Early in this period, your baby discovers his hands. At first he seems surprised when they wave into view, but later he examines them carefully as he does other objects. He also brings them to his face to explore his eyes, nose, cheeks and mouth. As he puts a rattle into his mouth, he sucks his fingers along with it. The sensations help him understand that the fingers are part of him and the rattle is not.

Emotional and Social

At three months, your baby probably bursts into smile at the approach of any adult. But soon he begins to recognize members of the family and becomes more discriminating in his responses. When someone familiar approaches, he may widen his eyes, pant, break out in a broad grin and wriggle his whole body in excited anticipation.

When he is unhappy, he can be soothed by your holding him, talking to him or just by the sight of your face, and this confidence is a sign of increasing trust. Toward the end of this period, he can become attached to a soft toy, blanket or other security object.

A baby almost four months old may be responsive to play for as much as an hour at a time. When he is ready for a game, he will let you know by vocalizing.

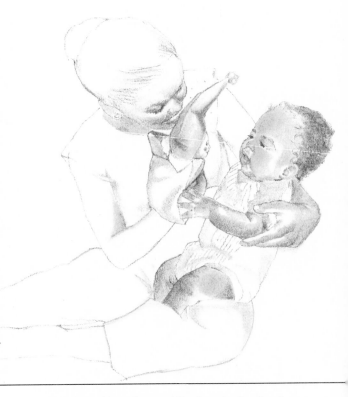

Listening to his mother providing the voice for a hand puppet, a three-month-old examines the toy both with his eyes and with a hand. Puppet play combines visual, verbal and motor development in a package that is pure fun. As the puppet closes in on the youngster, the next step is likely to be a tummy-tickle.

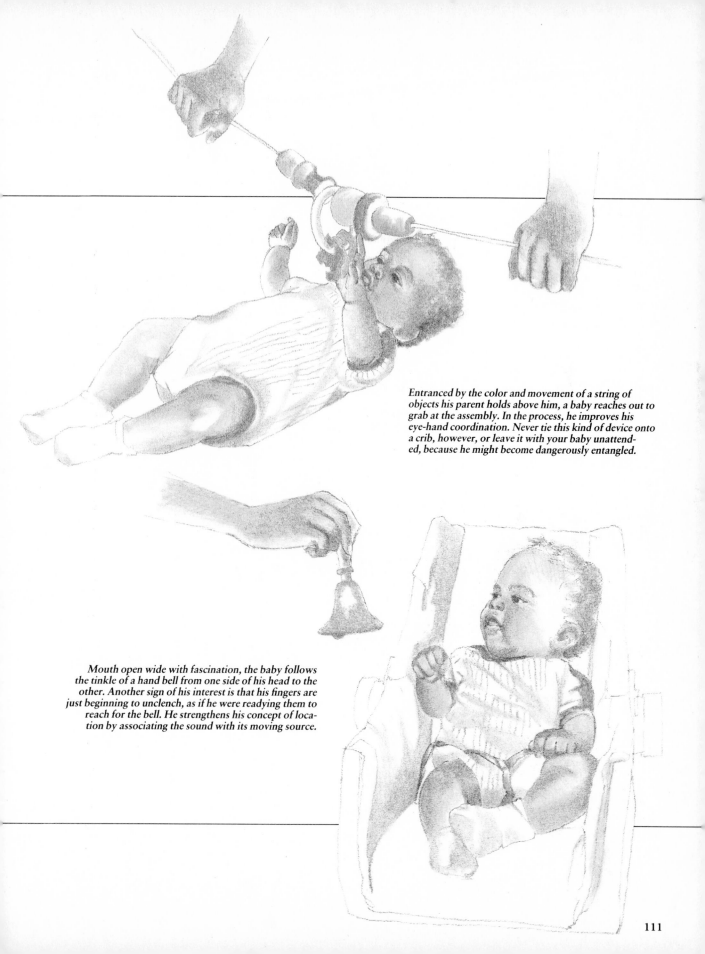

Entranced by the color and movement of a string of objects his parent holds above him, a baby reaches out to grab at the assembly. In the process, he improves his eye-hand coordination. Never tie this kind of device onto a crib, however, or leave it with your baby unattended, because he might become dangerously entangled.

Mouth open wide with fascination, the baby follows the tinkle of a hand bell from one side of his head to the other. Another sign of his interest is that his fingers are just beginning to unclench, as if he were readying them to reach for the bell. He strengthens his concept of location by associating the sound with its moving source.

111

Activities and Games

Muscle Control and Body Awareness

Beach ball rock Inflate a beach ball until it is almost full and then place your baby on top of it on his tummy. Hold him securely as you gently rock him back and forth, side to side, and round and

round in time to your singing or a recording. Start rolling him slowly and speed up the motion as he gets accustomed to it. He will soon begin to recognize when he should tighten his muscles in order to participate in maintaining his balance.

Inching forward You can help give your baby the chance to feel himself push forward, even before he learns to crawl. When you see him making pushing or swimming motions while lying on his tummy, press your hands firmly against the soles of his feet. He may push against your hands and inch forward. If he does not, try the exercise again at a later date.

Hearing and Language

Bell bracelets You can use the fascination of sound to increase your baby's awareness of his hands and feet. Tie a ribbon strung with one or more small jingling bells around his wrist. Lift his arm to shake the bell and make it ring. If he notices the tinkling sound, he may start moving his arm in order to make the bell ring. Try moving the bells from wrist to wrist and later to the ankles. Make sure the bells are securely fastened to the ribbons, so the baby cannot pull them off and swallow them. Remove the bells after five or 10 minutes.

More conversation Encourage your baby's language development by talking to him as much as possible. Describe what you are doing as you feed him, bathe him, clean his room. Name objects for him — especially those that he can handle, such as his bottle or a rattle. Hold up an item as you discuss it. Use his name often.

House tour Add a variation to your conversations with your baby by carrying him on tours of the house when he wishes to be held. Watch for the objects that seem to attract his attention because of their shapes, bright colors or sounds, and emphasize those in your talk. As during routine activities, describe what you are showing the child: "This is the faucet where we get our water. Listen to the hiss when the water runs." If your baby wants to touch the water, or anything else that will not harm him, encourage him to do so.

Vision and Perception

Picture gallery Babies enjoy looking at people or pictures of them, especially the people they are getting acquainted with. So if you do not already have a display of family photographs on a wall or table, create such a collection of large photos and introduce your child to it. Let him view the pictures frequently while you name the people in them. Let him touch the pictures if he wants to; although, of course, not in a manner that would endanger either the baby or the photographs.

Ring on a string Attach a shiny ring or another bright object to one end of a string. Place the baby in his infant seat and, holding the free end of the string above him, make the ring slowly circle the child's head at his eye level. Keep the ring circling in one direction and watch your baby's eyes as he learns to anticipate the predictable reappearance of the ring on one side of his head after it passes out of sight on the other side. The game will expose him to the regularity of objects in motion.

Bubble watch Babies who are old enough to see soap bubbles are usually fascinated by watching those iridescent spheres drift magically through the air. But this pastime also gives your child practice in tracking moving objects through eye and head movements. Take care to blow the bubbles away from your baby; a bubble bursting on his nose can startle the little one and the soap mixture can sting his eyes.

Shake play This simple game helps develop your baby's motor skills as well as vision judgment and the coordination between the two. Begin the exercise by putting into your baby's hand a toy that is easy to grasp and makes a noise when shaken, such as a rattle or an oversize play key ring. Shake that hand so the noise will attract the child's attention. See if he lifts the toy into his line of vision to discover what is creating the racket. If he does not, raise his arm for him and shake the toy again, while you talk to him about what is happening. Then try the other hand.

Emotional and Social

Giggle games By the time your baby is in his fourth month, he loves to play surprise tickle games. Chant a rhyme or any narrative in a sing-song voice: "The itsy bitsy spider . . ." and "Here comes a buzzy bee . . ." are two old favorites for developing his sense of humor. As you recite the litany, your fingers creep like a spider's or a bee's tiny, soft footsteps up the baby's arm or leg to a ticklish area such as his neck or midriff. Be careful as you deliver the coup de grâce, however: Too much tickling can overstimulate him and provoke confusion.

Riding a pony If you are typically loving and obliging parents, you and your spouse will be your child's "ponies" or "horsies" for many years to come. The baby will ride on your feet, knees, back and shoulders until both of you weari-

ly yearn to be turned out to pasture with Old Dobbin. There is value in your sacrifice, however. Your baby not only improves his capacity for social relationships by bonding tightly to these trustworthy mounts, but he develops his balance and muscle coordination as well. In the earliest stage, lie on your back, knees up. Place your baby securely on your lower legs, facing you, as you hold his hands in yours. Move your lower legs slowly up and down while you show your pleasure in the game with joyful facial gestures and by fixing your gaze on your child's eyes. And, as in almost all games that involve movement, sing a song at the same time.

For the Toy Box

A book or record of nursery rhymes to sing or recite when playing with your baby. Safe rattles and rings in various shapes. Hand puppets for parent-baby "dialogue." Rubber or cloth animals with squeaks or jingles securely fixed inside them. A plastic ball or cube with finger holes for the baby to grasp.

Months Five and Six

month	1	2	3	4	5	6	7	8	9	10	11	12

Your baby will become noticeably more active and alert as she moves through the fifth and sixth months of infancy. Now she will reach out and grasp things entirely on her own initiative, not just when you dangle them in front of her. Even when lying on her tummy, she will stretch to grab a toy out of easy reach. She babbles more and more, and with increasingly complex sounds. Her explorations and discoveries are very exciting to her, and she may spend up to two hours at a time happily playing, either with you or by herself. Although she may sleep through the night by now, she probably will awake at sunrise, eager to begin the day.

Muscle Control and Body Awareness

A baby's trunk and arm muscles continue strengthening during these months. When on her stomach, she props herself up on her sturdy arms for much longer periods than before. And now it is not only her head that moves from side to side; she will twist her whole torso to one side as she looks back over her shoulder at something behind her. Most babies love lying on their tummies, waving their arms and legs in a smoothly coordinated fashion like a swimmer practicing her strokes.

Soon your baby is rolling over so well, first from front to back and later from back to front, that she may use this new skill to travel across the floor. Or she may propel herself by scooting along, rocking and pivoting on her stomach. Babies of this age usually do not actually crawl yet, but some bend their knees and push themselves up into a crawling position, then stay there rocking back and forth.

Her increasing strength and coordination enable her to sit up briefly without any support, but she will probably topple to one side or the other within a few moments — though not before first trying to balance herself by planting her hands on the floor. If you pull her from a lying to a sitting position, she will help by drawing in her legs and bending at the waist. And when you lift her to a standing position and hold on to keep her from falling over, she may support her own weight, even bouncing up and down by flexing her legs.

When your baby uses her newfound agility to pick up an unfamiliar toy, she is determined to learn all about it — and at this age she knows that one way to do that is by putting it in her mouth and exploring it thoroughly with lips and tongue, turning it this way and that. Near the end of these two months, many children are able to transfer an object from one hand to the other.

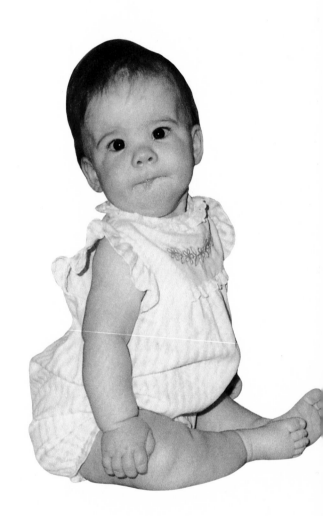

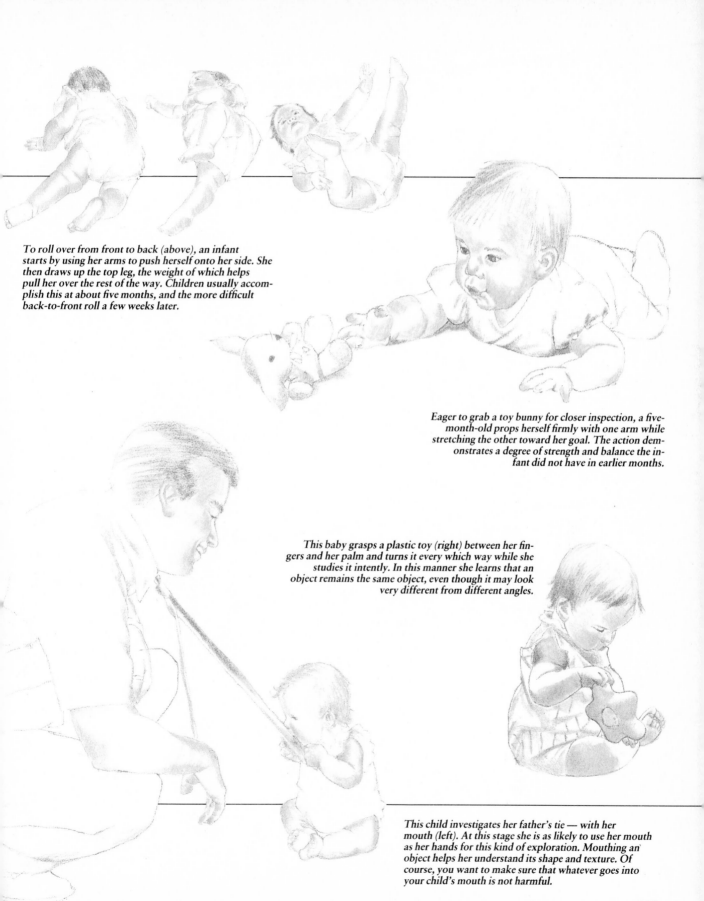

To roll over from front to back (above), an infant starts by using her arms to push herself onto her side. She then draws up the top leg, the weight of which helps pull her over the rest of the way. Children usually accomplish this at about five months, and the more difficult back-to-front roll a few weeks later.

Eager to grab a toy bunny for closer inspection, a five-month-old props herself firmly with one arm while stretching the other toward her goal. The action demonstrates a degree of strength and balance the infant did not have in earlier months.

This baby grasps a plastic toy (right) between her fingers and her palm and turns it every which way while she studies it intently. In this manner she learns that an object remains the same object, even though it may look very different from different angles.

This child investigates her father's tie — with her mouth (left). At this stage she is as likely to use her mouth as her hands for this kind of exploration. Mouthing an object helps her understand its shape and texture. Of course, you want to make sure that whatever goes into your child's mouth is not harmful.

Hearing and Language

Babies in their fifth and sixth months find their own sounds endlessly fascinating, and they begin to experiment with making all sorts of noises. For instance, your child may cough involuntarily and — intrigued by the sound of the cough — repeat it again and again.

Around this time, too, a baby's shapeless babbling will begin to take more definite form. Occasionally she will combine a consonant such as "b" or "d" with her airy vowels, producing a short string of syllables like "ba-ba-ba." If you imitate her sounds, she will probably stop to listen intently, then resume babbling even more enthusiastically. She learns to vary the rate, pitch and volume of her vocalizing. Most importantly, she begins to use language for a purpose, babbling to get your attention, for example.

Your baby enjoys other sounds, too, whether a pleasant voice or a song on the radio. Now she can distinguish each of several voices in a conversation around her. Upon hearing the sound of her name, she may turn her head to face the speaker. She also notices differences in tone and may frown or cry in response to an angry voice. And you may sometimes find her humming and swaying to music. By about six months of age, she laughs out loud when she is happy.

Vision and Perception

By the start of this period, an infant's eyesight is as sharp as an adult's. She sees things at varying distances and follows moving objects with both eyes. Your baby will use her newly improved vision to watch your face closely, and she may try to imitate your facial expressions.

Her eye-hand coordination continues to improve. Not only can she reach out and grasp toys she sees, she also can find her toes, grab them and bring them to her mouth.

Emotional and Social

Your baby is now quite a social being, devotedly attached to you but usually willing to relate to other people, although she may show some anxiety around strangers. She ceases to wait for you to initiate an exchange, now smiling or cooing first to let you know she wants to "talk" — or play, or snuggle. When you reach down to pick her up, she might even hold out her arms. This may seem a simple, predictable response, but it is an important sign that she is a full participant in the interaction between the two of you.

Her emotions are maturing. An infant of this age clearly displays disgust, fear and anger — all normal, healthy emotions — as well as the simple distress that not long before was the sole negative message in her emotional vocabulary. She conveys her feelings both with facial expressions and with sounds: disgusted grunts, contented gurgles and screeches of delight. She may express all of these in a mere half hour, for babies of this age go through rapid mood changes. An infant's tears can sometimes quickly be converted to laughter if you engage her lovingly and playfully.

Around this time, differences in baby personalities become more evident. One child may spend most of her waking hours lying quietly, looking around, handling toys and babbling softly to herself, while another might concentrate on vigorous physical activity, perhaps rolling over and over to travel across the floor.

A five-month-old protests the removal of a toy from her high-chair tray. Because a child of this age is so deeply absorbed in learning about the world, she becomes angry quickly when something she is studying — that is to say, something she is playing with — is taken away.

While her mother (above, right) watches with joy and pride, the five-month-old reveals in body language mixed feelings about the attention she is receiving from her mother's friend. Although the infant appears calm and willingly grasps the visitor's finger, her stiff, straightened legs indicate that she is experiencing some anxiety.

This baby tries to locate her rattle, which has just fallen to the floor beneath her walker. Having learned to follow moving objects by sight and sound, she now at last puts all the information together to trace something that drops from view. In earlier months, she would have been puzzled by a toy that vanished.

The baby delights in mirror play, smiling at her own reflection, although she may not realize she is seeing her own image. She can identify her mother's reflection but may think that the infant she sees is another child.

Activities and Games

Muscle Control and Body Awareness

Pull-ups *Place your infant on her back. Grasp her forearms and gently pull her up into a sitting position. She will assist you by bending her legs up out of the way, holding her head steady*

and leaning her trunk forward, strengthening neck, back and abdominal muscles.

Follow the toy *Use a toy to help your baby learn to roll from her back to her front. Lay her on her back and get her attention with a toy. (If she does not seem interested in it, postpone the game till another time.) Move the toy slowly in an arc to the side and top of her field of vision, so she will have to turn her head and shoulders and slightly arch her neck and back to keep the toy in sight. If the baby is developmentally ready to roll over, her effort to keep her eyes on the toy may cause her to do so. A gentle push on the backside may help. Even if the infant does not roll over, her muscles will benefit from the exercise.*

Reaching up *Seat your baby on the floor, surrounded by pillows in case she topples over. Then hold a toy just beyond her arm's reach, so that she has to straighten her back and stretch a little bit to get it. Give her the toy quickly, even if she does not quite reach it, so that she does not become frustrated. Reward her efforts with smiles and hugs. This game strengthens your infant's back while she practices both sitting on her own and reaching.*

Hearing and Language

A symphony of common sounds *Make sure your baby hears a wide variety of pleasing sounds. Let her crumple tissue paper to familiarize herself with the soft crackling noise — while you watch, to make sure she does not eat the paper. If it is autumn, carry her outdoors and rustle your feet through a pile of crisp leaves. Hit the bars of a toy xylophone or the keys of a piano. She will learn that sounds bring pleasure and that she can create them for herself.*

Rhythmic language *Although specific words probably mean little to her yet, your infant's response to the rhythm of language continues to develop. It is not too early to start reading to her briefly every day, from a book of Mother Goose or other nursery rhymes, for example.*

Babble dialogue *To encourage your baby's vocalization, imitate her sounds when she babbles. Wait until she pauses, then slowly repeat back to her one of her strings of syllables, such as "la-*

la-la." She probably will listen intently, then will either try to reproduce the sound or resume random babbling more enthusiastically than ever. Give her smiles and hugs to reinforce her efforts to imitate your imitation of her, but keep playing the game with her even if she does not repeat the original sound. Babies learn language through imitation, and eventually she will catch on.

Vision and Perception

Follow the bouncing ball To give your child yet more practice tracking moving objects with her eyes, play games with a brightly patterned ball — if possible, one that makes a noise. Roll it against a wall so that it comes spinning back. Slowly bounce it up and down. She will be exercising her visual skills while having fun.

Sights for new eyes Make sure your baby's environment is filled with interesting colors and shapes to look at. By this age, she is attracted to red and blue; try to provide them in her window shades, in posters on her walls or in her crib blankets. Keep moving her from room to room during the day. Childproof a space in the kitchen for her. Arrange for her to have time out of doors, on the porch or in the yard, so she will learn nature's special hues.

Now you see it . . . Start teaching your baby to look for things. Half-conceal a toy she likes beneath an overturned plastic bowl, leaving enough of the

toy showing for her to recognize it. Ask her where the toy is, and then help her to lift the bowl to find it. Act surprised and delighted that the toy has been uncovered. Once she has caught on, conceal the toy completely under the bowl or a towel, or slowly and obviously move it into hiding behind your back.

Emotional and Social

An expanding social life Continue to widen your child's circle of acquaintances — even if she does not remember many of them from one encounter to the next. Take her along when you visit friends. Share your guests with her. You should make an effort to introduce her to other children, but beware of exposing her to colds or other illnesses. By getting to know people outside the family, she is building social confidence even at this tender age.

Peekaboo There are many variations on this old favorite. It is probably best to start with the tamest, concealing Teddy or Dolly beneath a light baby blanket, then whipping off the cover as you exclaim "Peekaboo!" and laugh. Next you might progress to covering and uncovering

your eyes with your hands, then covering and uncovering your baby's eyes to the same peekaboo refrain. Keep it jolly so that she will know it is a game. If she seems to like it, try covering yourself with the blanket, then finally drape it over your baby. Besides giving the child a good time, you are helping her to learn that things and people continue to exist when they are out of sight.

For the Toy Box

Toys that make noise, such as rattles, squeaky squeeze toys, bells, a music box. Brightly colored balls. A baby's mirror. Stuffed animals. Toys with handles or loops that are easy to grasp. Safe kitchen measuring cups or ladles.

Months Seven and Eight

month	1	2	3	4	5	6	7	8	9	10	11	12

Probably the most important development in these two months is your baby's increasing ability to move around. No longer satisfied to investigate only what is brought to him, he will start to creep or crawl purposefully toward whatever attracts his attention. His emerging mobility is both exhilarating and frightening for him. He may assert his independence one day and cling to you the next. Paradoxically, as he develops the physical skill to move away from you, he feels his dependence and the need for love more than ever.

Muscle Control and Body Awareness

As the baby's trunk muscles grow ever stronger, he spends less and less time lying on his back and stomach. By the end of this period, he can sit unsupported for as long as he likes. At six months he may need to be placed in the sitting position, but at eight months he will be able to get there himself, either from his side or from all fours. And he will be able to remain sitting up while pivoting to get a toy, bouncing up and down on his bottom, or scooting across a room.

Muscular development reaches the legs and feet during these two months. When the baby is lying on his back, he may kick vigorously, relishing the smack of his feet on the floor. He may use these kicks together with a squirming motion to move a considerable distance. Or, he may propel himself by creeping on his stomach, using his arms to pull the rest of his body forward. Later in this period, he will probably crawl on all fours. But before mastering this motion, he may go through a period of a few days or even weeks during which he gets up on his hands and knees and rocks back and forth. Some babies do very little crawling, but manage to get around during these months by one of the other methods.

With greater leg strength, the baby does more of the work when you help him to a stand, and he bears his own weight once on his feet. Although he can keep his legs straight, he may prefer to bob up and down. By the end of these two months, he may try to pull himself to a stand while holding onto a piece of furniture. It will take him some time and a few backward tumbles before he accomplishes this.

Learning to stand is a major achievement for a baby. Once he is able to do it, he will try pulling himself up on any available piece of furniture. Some very active babies will even try to move along short distances using tentative sideways steps while holding onto furniture. At this stage, however, he may not yet know how to get back down from a standing position and will cry out for help. Release his hands from whatever they are gripping and lower him gently onto his bottom.

As in earlier months, the baby will reach for and examine objects of all kinds and put them into his mouth for further testing. But now he learns to use his thumb separately from his fingers, as an opposable digit, and thus can grasp things between thumb and fingers. Because of this, he can hold onto a toy for a long period, smoothly passing it back and forth between his hands in order to inspect its properties thoroughly. While playing with a toy, the baby may shake it up and down, then bang it on the floor, delighted by the effect of his own actions. Some children may be able to grasp an object in each hand and bang them together. By the end of this period, many will be able to hold their own bottles, and some may even handle and drink from a training cup with a spouted cap.

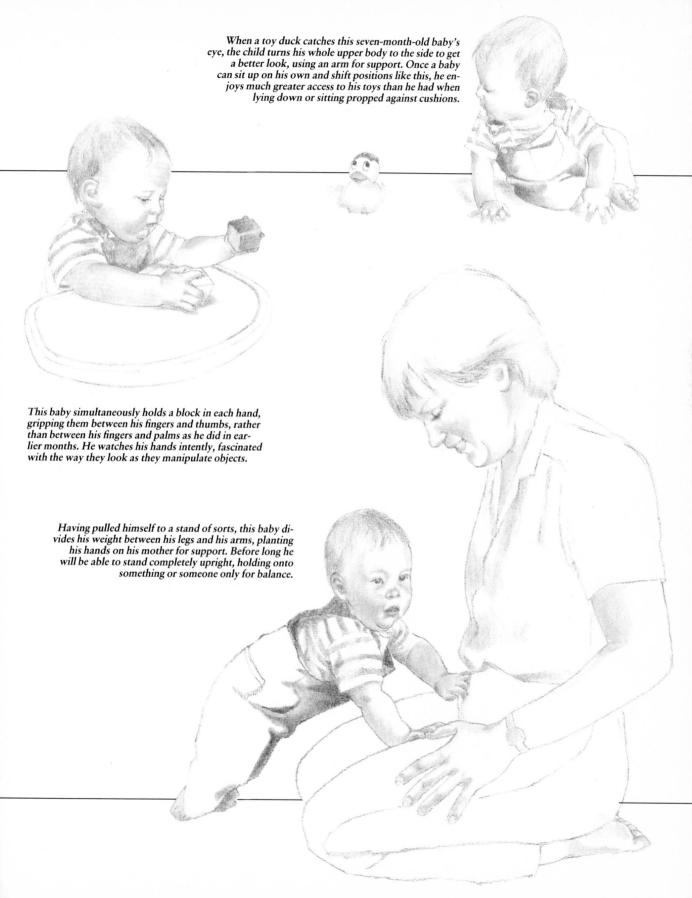

When a toy duck catches this seven-month-old baby's eye, the child turns his whole upper body to the side to get a better look, using an arm for support. Once a baby can sit up on his own and shift positions like this, he enjoys much greater access to his toys than he had when lying down or sitting propped against cushions.

This baby simultaneously holds a block in each hand, gripping them between his fingers and thumbs, rather than between his fingers and palms as he did in earlier months. He watches his hands intently, fascinated with the way they look as they manipulate objects.

Having pulled himself to a stand of sorts, this baby divides his weight between his legs and his arms, planting his hands on his mother for support. Before long he will be able to stand completely upright, holding onto something or someone only for balance.

Hearing and Language

By the time your baby is in his seventh and eighth months, he is well aware of the differences in the many sounds, familiar and unfamiliar, that attract his attention. The child may interrupt his play and turn his head inquisitively at noises ranging from the ringing of a telephone to the roaring of a truck, and he has an easier time locating the source of the sound than in earlier months.

When you speak to your baby, you may notice him watching you closely: He is studying the movements of your mouth and jaw. If you feed him back one of his strings of syllables — "da-da-da" — he may studiously try to imitate your mouth and jaw movements as he repeats the sounds. He continues to respond mainly to the speaker's tone of voice, rather than to the meanings of the words themselves, but by the end of this period your child will probably understand a few words and can pick out his name when he hears it in a conversation, turning to the person who said it.

Vision and Perception

Children of this age show great interest in small objects, eagerly pursuing bits of dust and crumbs of food even though they have difficulty picking them up. During these months, the baby learns to compare visually large and small objects, gathering information that helps him adjust his grasp according to the size of an item. He sees detail well and is curious about designs and patterns. Don't be surprised if one day you observe your little one trying hard to lift an illustration off a page in a book: While the child sees the object pictured quite clearly, he does not yet understand the difference between two and three dimensions.

In these months, the baby tests the effects of his actions on objects by deliberately dropping his toys — often in rapid succession — and following the motion with his eyes. He also enjoys having a container full of small toys that he can gleefully dump out; in the process he gains experience that will lead to an understanding of in and out, full and empty. Because the baby now has an accurate mental picture of how a familiar room usually appears, he can be surprised or even uneasy when he notices a change — a table that has been pushed aside for his own safety, for example. And since he is moving about now, your child's perception of the distance between himself and an object is improving.

Emotional and Social

Observing, imitating and patting you and others, the baby continues to show great interest in people. By now, however, he discriminates much more sharply between family and strangers; children of this age show varying degrees of anxiety around unknown people. In the presence of a stranger, your little one may remain calm as long as you are with him, but cry when you leave. He may be clingy and dependent even when you are alone with him, since his increasing mobility often makes his world seem unstable. He is learning that he is separate from you, and this sometimes upsets him.

Your child is developing a stronger sense of himself as an individual with particular likes and dislikes. He will resist your suggestions at times and push away a toy that does not interest him, or shout to get one he does want. He may explore all the parts of his body with great curiosity. And he may test his power over you by crying for you helplessly, then giggling when you appear at his side. In spite of his new anxieties during these two months, the baby enjoys playing by himself as well as interacting with others. A broad smile from you will often elicit a big grin in response, and a favorite game may send the baby into peals of laughter.

The seven-month-old's pleasure in drinking from a cup reveals his enjoyment of his emerging independence — a quality he will want to exercise by feeding himself crackers and bits of food as well.

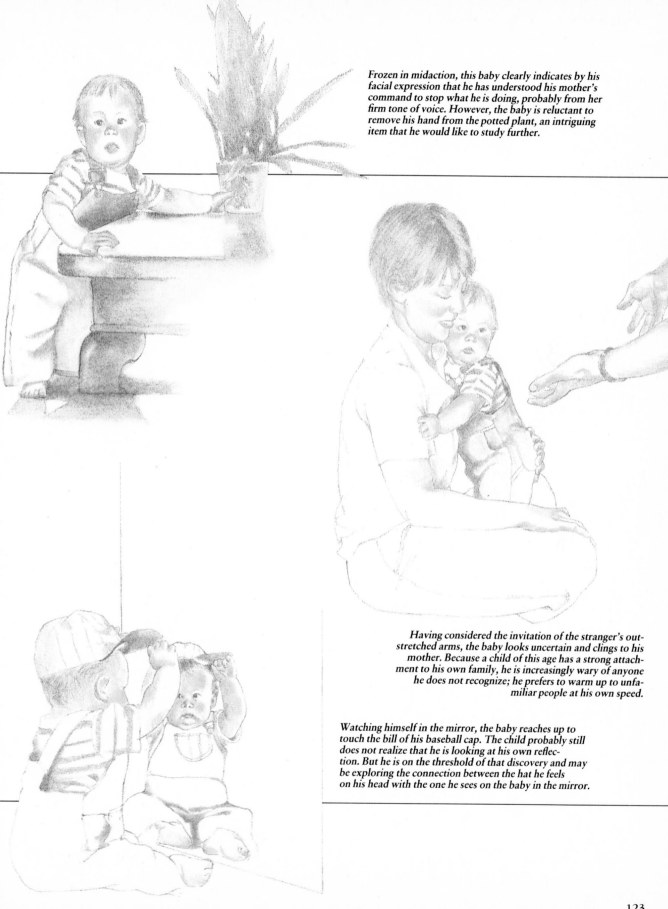

Frozen in midaction, this baby clearly indicates by his facial expression that he has understood his mother's command to stop what he is doing, probably from her firm tone of voice. However, the baby is reluctant to remove his hand from the potted plant, an intriguing item that he would like to study further.

Having considered the invitation of the stranger's outstretched arms, the baby looks uncertain and clings to his mother. Because a child of this age has a strong attachment to his own family, he is increasingly wary of anyone he does not recognize; he prefers to warm up to unfamiliar people at his own speed.

Watching himself in the mirror, the baby reaches up to touch the bill of his baseball cap. The child probably still does not realize that he is looking at his own reflection. But he is on the threshold of that discovery and may be exploring the connection between the hat he feels on his head with the one he sees on the baby in the mirror.

Activities and Games

Muscle Control and Body Awareness

Tunnel travel *A tunnel made from a large cardboard box provides your little one an incentive to crawl as well as a chance to experience firsthand the difference between inside and outside. Remove the flaps from the box or fold them inside. Then place the baby near one end of the tunnel and seat yourself on the floor at the other*

end. Encourage the baby to crawl through the tunnel to reach you.

Stand-ups *To show the baby that he can reach things by standing up, place an inviting toy on the seat of a sturdy chair. Try to suggest by words and movements that he get the toy by pulling himself up, holding onto the chair. If he has trouble doing it or does not understand, help him to his feet and lean him against the chair so he can reach the toy.*

Getting a third toy *This exercise helps the baby learn to release one toy to get another. While he has a toy in each hand, put another in front of him and call his attention to it. At first he may reach with the toy still in his hand. Later he will discover how to drop one to get another.*

Pick-up *To give your child practice in picking up objects of different sizes and shapes, float small toys in his bath, place pieces of food on his high-chair tray and provide him with a variety of objects to play with.*

Hearing and Language

Outdoor sounds *This outdoor activity complements the baby's own interest in tracking sounds. When you hear an airplane, a barking dog, a cawing crow, a roaring truck, turn your child toward the source of the sound and point it out. Then imitate the noise and name the source. As well as learning to locate sounds, the baby will find out what makes them.*

An ear for music *Records of all kinds of music — as well as wind-up music boxes and other musical toys — find a willing audience in most children. Put on a lullaby before bedtime, a rousing march before a walk, a polka while dancing your baby around the room.*

Hidden sounds *A squeak toy can help the baby learn to use sound to locate objects that are out of sight. Begin by showing him a toy that squeaks. Squeeze it, then hide it under a soft cloth and squeak it again. Ask the baby where the noise came from and help him find the toy.*

Baby talk *Continue to talk to your baby often, using short, simple sentences. Speak about the present and be concrete. Use the names of objects and people repeatedly instead of substituting pronouns such as "it" and "them." Babies have short memories and cannot think abstractly. To help the baby understand, use exaggerated gestures when appropriate. Although he cannot respond verbally yet, he is listening and learning to associate words with objects, events and people.*

Vision and Perception

Pat-a-cake *This traditional game teaches the baby to imitate gestures. Begin by patting the child's hands together as you sing the rhyme. After a few rounds, start clapping your hands as the baby watches or puts his hands on yours. Then invite him to clap as you sing. It may take the little one a while to learn how to clap on his own, so be patient.*

In and out *Your baby probably likes to dump things out of a container, but he may not be able to put them back. Fill a plastic bucket with small toys and let the baby dump them out. Keep refilling the bucket as long as he is interested.*

Pull the toy *A six- or seven-month-old probably can begin to understand how to use one object to get another. Tie a string around one of the baby's favorite toys and place the toy itself beyond the baby's reach, leaving the end of the string in front of him. Then show the baby that he can get the toy by pulling the string. Remember always to remove the string before leaving the toy alone with the baby.*

Emotional and Social

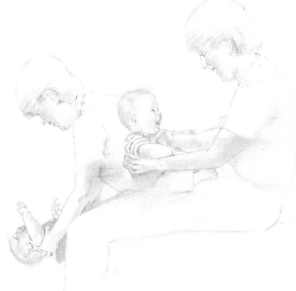

Knee-drops *This playful game teaches your baby to anticipate actions. Place him on your lap. Hold him firmly around his chest and gently bounce him up and down, singing a simple song such as "Row, Row, Row Your Boat." On the last phrase of a verse, lower him between your knees and laugh. After a few days, he may show you he knows what is coming by tensing his muscles or laughing first.*

Tug-of-war *An old-fashioned tug-of-war game teaches the baby about taking turns. Give your child one end of a scarf and take the other end yourself. Pull gently on your end, then release it and see if the baby will take a turn tugging at his end. If not, place your other hand over his and show him how to pull.*

Saying good-by *If your child cries when you leave him, help him understand that you always return. Even when you are leaving for a short time, say "bye-bye," and tell him you will be right back. Then return within a few minutes so he will quickly discover you have not disappeared permanently. Gradually increase the period of time when you are gone.*

For the Toy Box

Toys that the baby can make react: squeak toys, suction-cup toys, rattles. Several hats to try on in front of the mirror. Balls for the crawling baby to roll and push. Sieves, plastic cups, a baster and a funnel for bathtub play.

Months Nine and 10

month	1	2	3	4	5	6	7	8	9	10	11	12

You will probably be amazed at your baby's mobility and coordination during these two months. He crawls rapidly and smoothly and will even venture far enough from your side to explore the next room. His once-tentative attempts to stand are nearly always successful these days, and he is starting to take a few steps sideways while holding onto furniture or his playpen for support. The baby's powers of concentration have expanded to match his physical development. He will pursue a game or play with a toy persistently, ignoring distractions. And his developing memory means that he is less patient now with repetitive games.

Muscle Control and Body Awareness

Crawling now is almost certainly the baby's chief form of locomotion. He can turn around to reverse direction when necessary, crawl while holding a toy in one hand and may crawl on straightened limbs, a precursor to walking. Some babies will start crawling up steps during this period, so stay close when your child is near a stairway. Going down stairs is usually too difficult for a baby of this age.

With better control over his legs and feet than in earlier months, your baby may be able to stand unsupported for a few moments. When holding onto something for support, he is confident enough to let go with one hand in order to turn to the side or even to crouch down to pick up a toy. Sitting down from a standing position, a skill that may have eluded your baby previously, will become increasingly easy during these two months. And the baby enters the prewalking stage known as cruising — taking small sideways steps while holding onto furniture for balance. If you hold him securely under the arms, he may take a few forward steps.

Your child's control over his hands and fingers has kept pace with his other physical achievements. Now he may be able to bang one object while running the fingers of his other hand over another, demonstrating considerable coordination. And the baby can keep his grip on one object while reaching for a second one. He is learning to use each finger separately and can pick up objects between his thumb and index finger, so small items no longer escape his grasp. Still somewhat awkward at releasing objects, he may throw or drop them when he loses interest. With his newfound dexterity, your baby probably cannot resist poking his index finger into every nook and cranny, including into your ears and nostrils, to better explore his surroundings.

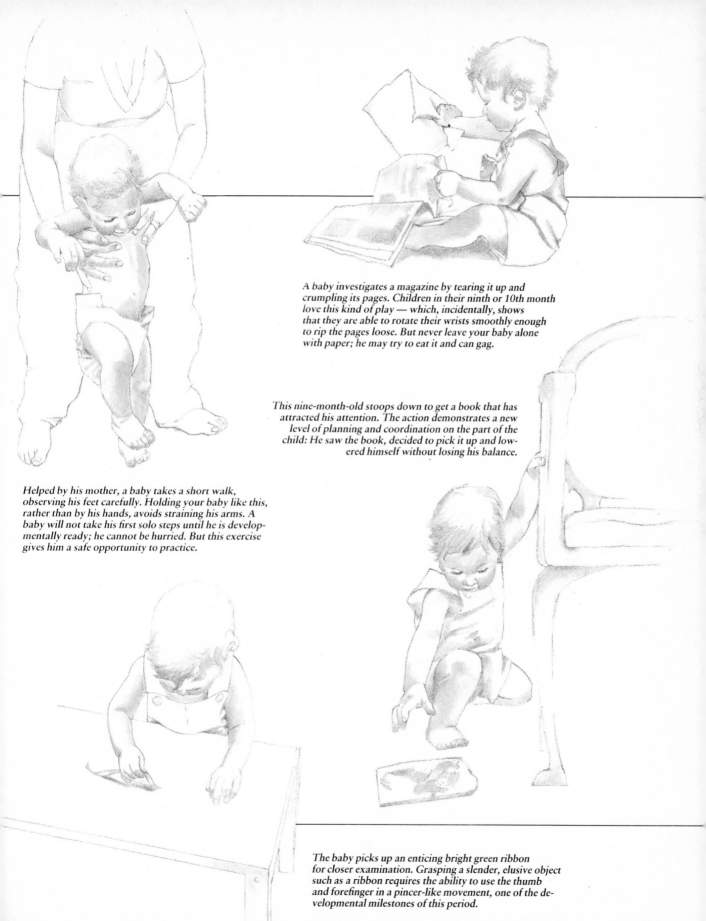

A baby investigates a magazine by tearing it up and crumpling its pages. Children in their ninth or 10th month love this kind of play — which, incidentally, shows that they are able to rotate their wrists smoothly enough to rip the pages loose. But never leave your baby alone with paper; he may try to eat it and can gag.

This nine-month-old stoops down to get a book that has attracted his attention. The action demonstrates a new level of planning and coordination on the part of the child: He saw the book, decided to pick it up and lowered himself without losing his balance.

Helped by his mother, a baby takes a short walk, observing his feet carefully. Holding your baby like this, rather than by his hands, avoids straining his arms. A baby will not take his first solo steps until he is developmentally ready; he cannot be hurried. But this exercise gives him a safe opportunity to practice.

The baby picks up an enticing bright green ribbon for closer examination. Grasping a slender, elusive object such as a ribbon requires the ability to use the thumb and forefinger in a pincer-like movement, one of the developmental milestones of this period.

127

Hearing and Language

In the ninth and 10th months, you will hear more two-syllable sounds than previously, and perhaps a few real words such as "mama" and "dada." Your baby will have little comprehension of these words when he first says them, but within a few months, he will probably have a good idea of their meaning. Babies of this age also begin to make what child development authorities call pseudo-conversation, babbling with the intonations of adult speech, although few recognizable words are uttered. Through this kind of babble, the baby shows that he can vary pitch, rate and volume in imitation of what he hears.

A few familiar words will get a response from the baby around this time. With eye contact and smiles he lets you know that he clearly recognizes his name. By stopping an action he shows that he understands "no-no." He may wave "bye-bye" when you ask him to. At 10 months the baby may respond to a command involving one simple action — "Give me the ball," for example. And throughout this period his interest in sounds of all sorts continues. He loves to listen to you click your tongue or cough, and he will copy you as best he can.

Vision and Perception

By now, the baby has learned quite a bit about the visual world. He understands the concepts of up and down, and consequently, he may suddenly become afraid to try to get down from a low chair he has climbed onto. When he rights an upside-down cup, he demonstrates his recognition of the object's normal appearance. He also becomes much more proficient at roughly determining the size of something, which gives him more skill in grasping objects. This improved eye-hand coordination means that most babies of this age can bang two blocks together in front of their bodies and drop items into a container.

If you hide something where it is slightly difficult to get, such as under a pillow, your baby persists in his search instead of losing interest, as he might have done earlier. He finally fully understands that an object continues to exist even when he cannot see it. His comprehension is not complete, however; if he sees you hide the toy under another cushion, he may become confused and search for it again beneath the first.

During these months, the child continues to sharpen his sense of what things look like. He moves his toys up and down, away from and toward his face, turns them upside down, and he squints his eyes to get still another view.

Emotional and Social

Around this time, babies may start to be afraid of events that previously did not disturb them — taking a bath or visiting a strange place, for example. This is natural, since they are becoming more conscious of themselves as separate entities and are developing concerns for their own well-being. The baby's emerging sense of self also means that sometimes he may protest loudly if you stop him from doing what he wants to do.

As the baby matures, his interest in people grows. He loves to play games with you and will take the initiative more and more, grabbing your hands to elicit a round of pat-a-cake, for instance. This is an important development, because the most productive learning exchanges between parent and child are those the child initiates. And he is turning into quite a ham, gleefully showing off when he has an appreciative audience. Other people's moods now have more effect on the baby: He may be excited when you are or start to cry if he sees another baby in tears. Because he knows both you and himself better, he is even more likely than before to be wary of strangers and may look to you for reassurance when someone new approaches him. Yet his attachment to favorite cuddly toys indicates his capacity to extend affection beyond you, a healthy development.

Eager to practice his independence, a baby enjoys feeding himself food in small bite-size pieces — although you should keep an eye on him in case he gags or chokes on the food. Mealtime will probably be most pleasurable if you allow your child to alternate his self-feeding with your spoonfuls.

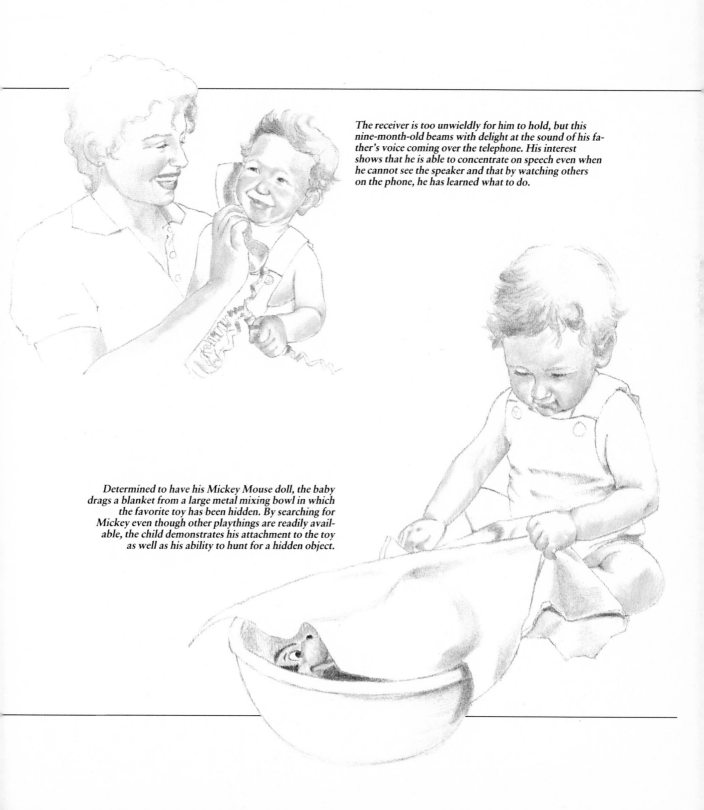

The receiver is too unwieldly for him to hold, but this nine-month-old beams with delight at the sound of his father's voice coming over the telephone. His interest shows that he is able to concentrate on speech even when he cannot see the speaker and that by watching others on the phone, he has learned what to do.

Determined to have his Mickey Mouse doll, the baby drags a blanket from a large metal mixing bowl in which the favorite toy has been hidden. By searching for Mickey even though other playthings are readily available, the child demonstrates his attachment to the toy as well as his ability to hunt for a hidden object.

Activities and Games

Muscle Control and Body Awareness

Poker *This game caters to your baby's delight in poking his forefinger into small places. Glue different fabrics and hard foods — fur, silk and uncooked macaroni — into the hollows of an empty egg carton. Show the baby how to stroke or probe each substance. Talk to him about how it feels. Stay with the baby to prevent him from pulling anything loose and putting it into his mouth.*

Letting go *Dropping blocks into a metal dish makes a satisfying clink and helps your child improve*

his ability to release objects. Pick up the block, show it to your baby, then turn your hand palm-down and splay your fingers broadly when you drop the block, so the child can plainly see the action. He may develop his own technique for releasing the block, such as pressing his hand against the dish. Do not pressure the baby. The game should be fun even when the child misses or just taps the block against the bowl.

Cruise line *Place heavy, stable chairs side by side in a row to create a line of support for your baby when he cruises. To encourage him to step along the whole row, move a favorite toy from one chair to the next, or put different toys on each chair and point them out to the baby one by one, as he progresses along the row. You should always supervise your child's use of his cruise line; he might tumble and pull a chair over onto himself.*

Hearing and Language

Knees and nose *Make up songs or rhymes that name parts of your baby's body and their functions. Sing or chant them to the baby when you bathe him or when he is observing himself in the mirror. The child will begin to recognize the terms for parts of his body.*

Naming toys *Place two familiar toys in front of your baby one at a time and name them. Then ask him to show you the one that you now name: "Show me the Teddy bear." Accept any response — touching, reaching or simply looking at the toy. Say something like "Yes, you looked at Teddy." If the child does not respond at all to your request, hand him the correct toy and repeat its name.*

Book talk *Reading simple picture books with your child will reinforce his understanding of familiar words and teach him some new ones. As you slowly turn the pages, tell him the name of whatever is pictured. Sometimes say what it is used for, or where the child might see it in real life. Choose sturdy books that have one large illustration on each page.*

Tube messages *This game will capture your baby's attention and give him a chance to listen closely to your voice. Send him sound messages — words and funny noises — through a long cardboard tube. Give the child the tube and show him how to speak through it. The tube concentrates sound, so you should speak softly and leave a small space between its end and your baby's ear.*

Vision and Perception

Copycat *Encouraging the baby to copy simple, enjoyable actions will help him learn through imitation. Try banging a wooden spoon on a metal pot, then letting him be the drummer.*

Or, while sitting in front of the child, touch one of your feet, or open and close a hand, or rock back and forth. Encourage your baby to copy what you do.

Upside down *This exercise will give your child practice in looking at things from different angles. Turn a toy upside down and place it in front of him. See if he turns it right side up. If he does not, show him how to do it a few times.*

So big *There is something infectious about this simple game, which introduces the baby to his own size. Ask your child how big he is. Then spread your arms wide to show him and say, "So big." If you keep repeating the game occasionally, the child eventually will stretch his arms in imitation of you.*

Emotional and Social

Hide-and-seek *This perennial favorite, an advanced version of the hide-the-toy games you have been playing with your child, will accustom him to surprises and the thrill of discovery. Crouch down out of sight — say, behind a sofa. Call your child's name and peek around the corner of the couch to give him a visual hint. Then duck back out of sight and call again. Maintain verbal contact as he crawls to you. When you are discovered, laugh, shout "You found me!" and reward him with a hug.*

Shelf space *Give the baby a low shelf in his room or the family room for some of his toys. Being able to get his own toys while you are busy will encourage his sense of independence.*

Fun in the tub *Nurture your child's playful spirit in the bath. Blow bubbles with a straw, make rain with a sieve, teach him to splash.*

Catch me *This game teaches your baby how to follow you so he will be able to keep you in sight when he wants to. Crawl a short distance from him, then turn around and say, "Come get me." Let him catch you. Then laugh, hug your baby and crawl away again.*

For the Toy Box

A round spindle with rings of graduated sizes to stack on it. A widemouthed plastic container filled with blocks. To create homemade music: an old pot and an empty cardboard box to beat on, a wooden spoon or two and an aluminum pie plate with bells securely attached to it.

Months 11 and 12

| month | 1 | 2 | 3 | 4 | 5 | 6 | 7 | 8 | 9 | 10 | 11 | 12 |

During these months, a baby makes her biggest strides yet toward independence. Almost a toddler, she may even take her first few steps alone. She is especially eager to communicate, often speaking in her own gibberish sprinkled with familiar words and sounds. She is curious about everything, and she will try scribbling with crayons, and feeding and dressing herself. The world no longer revolves around the baby; rather, the baby begins to see herself as part of a larger world filled with her toys, family members and all kinds of everyday challenges such as finding a lost ball or stacking a set of blocks.

At the same time, however, your child still depends heavily on you for love and attention. She actually may fear separation from you more than before, almost as if she foresees that her days of pure dependency on you are coming to an end. But always keep in mind that children develop at different rates. If your child turns one year old without taking a step or drinking from a cup, do not be concerned. Emphasize the gains she has made and encourage her to continue trying new things.

Muscle Control and Body Awareness

A child's most noticeable muscle control advance during these months is her progress toward walking. If she is not already taking sideways steps while holding onto furniture, she probably will start during this period. Soon after that, she will try to take a few forward steps while holding your hand. Later, she may try on her own, although many children do not perfect their walking skills until they are 18 months old. Once she starts moving on her own two feet, she becomes so fascinated by her accomplishment that she may not want to sit down anymore. For the time being, taking steps is more fun than any of her toys.

Babies approaching their first birthdays often demonstrate mastery of other physical feats, too — climbing, squatting, pivoting and sitting down easily. Around this time, they usually gain more skill in purposefully releasing objects held in their hands, an awkward exercise until now.

Perhaps most significant, your baby consistently links her actions to specific goals. If she wants the ball in the corner, she crawls after it. To take a bite, she raises her spoon to her mouth — with a little help from you, at first. She reaches inside a box to get a toy. Her dexterity improves daily. You can help by challenging her with games and exercises and letting her do as much as possible for herself. If she wants a certain toy, let her reach or crawl for it instead of handing it to her. The struggle makes her view the toy as a reward and getting it as a triumph.

Ever curious and intermittently intrepid, a baby climbs the stairs (right) to see what is going on above. From now on, she will be using her improved mobility to explore. You will have to keep a close watch on her, until you are sure she can get safely up and down stairs and that all areas she can get to are babyproof.

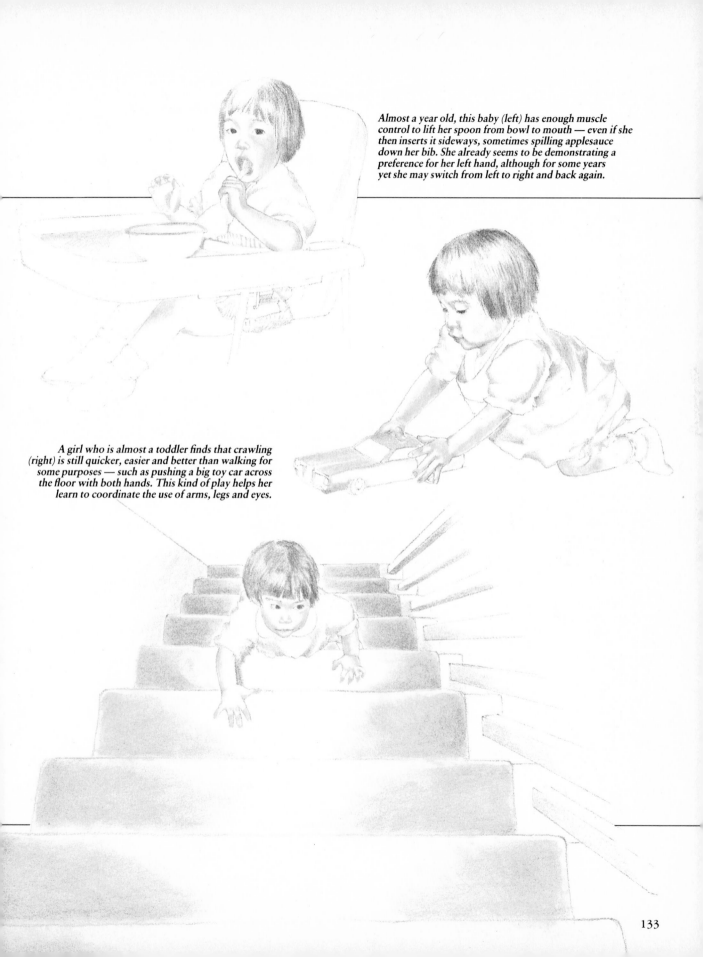

Almost a year old, this baby (left) has enough muscle control to lift her spoon from bowl to mouth — even if she then inserts it sideways, sometimes spilling applesauce down her bib. She already seems to be demonstrating a preference for her left hand, although for some years yet she may switch from left to right and back again.

A girl who is almost a toddler finds that crawling (right) is still quicker, easier and better than walking for some purposes — such as pushing a big toy car across the floor with both hands. This kind of play helps her learn to coordinate the use of arms, legs and eyes.

Hearing and Language

The babbling of a baby of this age is progressing to the point where some of what she says is intelligible. During this period, she may use several words frequently, including such common early words as "mama," "cookie" and "doggie." When you name an object, she may point to it or the place where she would expect to find it, even if she cannot say the word. An 11-month-old likes to imitate everything — your words, your facial gestures and intonations, animal sounds. The more words she hears and the more often she hears them, the more associations she will make. If she hears "cup" every time she has a drink, she learns the connection between the actual cup and its name.

And she is learning that she, too, can issue those important command words that have played such a big role in adult communication with her. She may begin to say "no" at every opportunity, even when she really means yes. Later, she will be more selective, declaring "no" along with a vigorous shake of the head when offered a snack she does not like.

In short, she is realizing that language allows her to make her wishes known, sharpening her sense of self as an independent person. She is becoming a participant rather than an observer in her world, which is expanding along with her vocabulary.

Vision and Perception

As a baby becomes more agile and more mobile, she begins to see her environment in many dimensions — up and down, in and out, near and far, big and small. All that climbing and standing is giving her a much sharper perception of space and distance than she had before. She now sees objects as existing separately from her and in many contexts, and they fascinate her endlessly. She discovers that a ball can be thrown, hidden, dropped and manipulated in lots of other ways. Her more highly developed eye-hand coordination skills allow her to begin to stack large blocks and to put small boxes inside bigger ones.

Your baby's memory is also improving. She may now remember where toys and other objects are normally found. She may be able to group objects by shape and color. Her attention span is increasing, and she will study pictures in books intently and may make her own scribblings. She is still confused, however, by glass and mirrors, and she may try to reach through them now and again to grasp an object. After a little more experience with glass, she will learn that it is a bit trickier than other materials, and she will adapt. Your baby's ability to make such distinc-

tions and to manipulate objects is part of a very important process: She is learning how to think, how to solve problems.

Emotional and Social

This is a confusing time emotionally for your baby. As her motor skills improve, enabling her to be increasingly independent physically, and as she becomes more acutely aware of herself as a separate entity, she may cling to you even more than before. She realizes that she can separate herself from you now, and that scares her. She may frequently need to take a break from her games to climb on your lap for reassurance.

Your baby is also learning to express her emotions consciously now, and while her new sense of humor and demonstrations of affection may be charming, her angry episodes in response to frustration are not. Stay calm and do not give in to her demands. She is learning what is acceptable behavior and what is not, and she may try to test your limits. A firm "no" will let her know when you disapprove. You will also see your baby becoming more sociable. She takes a greater interest in other family members and begins to play contentedly alongside — but not yet with — other children. This parallel play is a natural preliminary to play in which your child will interact with other children.

Concentrating in a way that would have been impossible a few months ago, an 11-month-old stacks blocks. At this age, much of her play involves problem-solving. She may arrange objects by color or size, but because she cannot understand the words for those abstractions, she cannot yet follow direction regarding color or size.

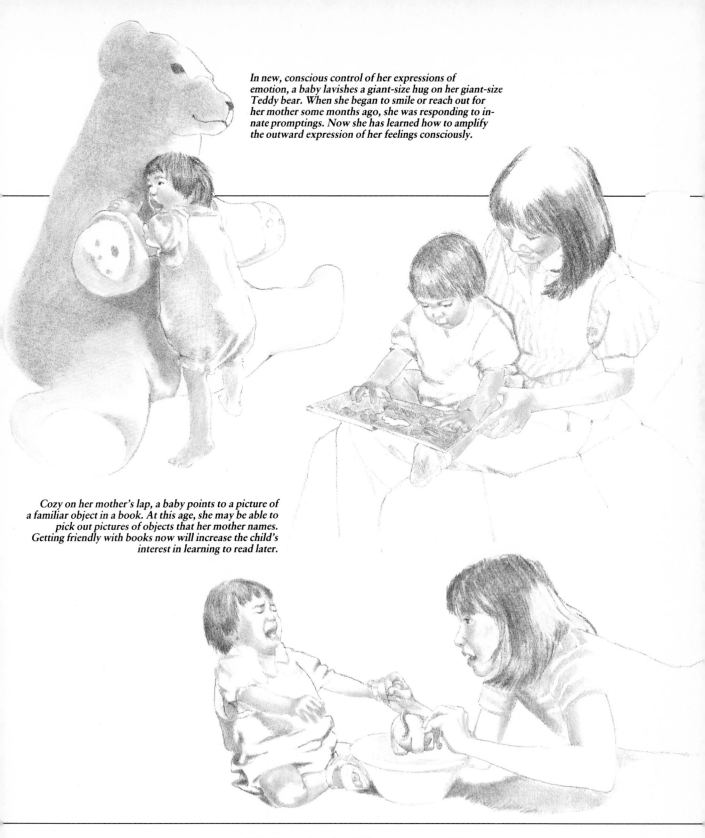

In new, conscious control of her expressions of emotion, a baby lavishes a giant-size hug on her giant-size Teddy bear. When she began to smile or reach out for her mother some months ago, she was responding to innate promptings. Now she has learned how to amplify the outward expression of her feelings consciously.

Cozy on her mother's lap, a baby points to a picture of a familiar object in a book. At this age, she may be able to pick out pictures of objects that her mother names. Getting friendly with books now will increase the child's interest in learning to read later.

When her mother tries to take a toy away in order to get her ready for bed, the baby howls in protest, using her new control of emotional display in an attempt to persuade her mother to give in to her demands. Her mother remains calm but firm, knowing the child must learn that she cannot always have her way.

135

Activities and Games

Muscle Control and Body Awareness

Baby basketball This game improves your baby's coordination. Give her a beanbag or a ball and let her drop it or throw it into a laundry basket or bucket. Demonstrate by dropping the beanbag into the bucket yourself.

Going barefoot Let your baby walk barefoot on different surfaces — sand, soft grass, a wooden deck, a cold tile floor — to increase her awareness of textures. If she shows a dislike for a strange surface, introduce different textures to her slowly by letting her sit on your lap while she dangles her feet onto the surface.

Stomach slide Once a baby learns to climb stairs, it is time to learn to climb back down safely. Teach your baby to slide gently down the stairs on her stomach, feet first. This activity is good for her coordination. Of course, continue to supervise her whenever she is on the stairs.

Crawling the plank Help your baby improve her balance by letting her crawl — or, if she can, walk — the plank. Place a smooth board (an ironing board will do) flat on the floor with a toy or stuffed animal at one end. The board should be at least four feet long and six inches wide. While you stay nearby, encourage your little one to crawl along the board to get the toy.

Stroller push Let a baby who can walk push her own stroller. She will enjoy it, and it will improve her stability and balance. Stay close to make sure the stroller does not roll too fast. If the child gets tired, she can always ride.

Hearing and Language

Where is . . .? To reinforce and expand your child's understanding of words, point out objects, family members, or parts of your or her body to her, and repeat their names several times. Then

ask, "Where is Mommy's nose?" (Or ask her about her own nose or the cup or Daddy.) If she does not point to it, show her where it is. Teaching her the names of body parts will also develop her self-awareness.

Story time Although your baby cannot yet follow a story, she loves going through picture books with you. Encourage her to point out familiar objects, but do not be surprised if she has trouble at first recognizing something she knows only in its three-dimensional form. Keep repeating the names of new objects and animals as you point them out. This is very important: It teaches her to identify objects with names and helps foster a love for books.

"Hi" and "Bye" With practice, your baby can learn these two words, probably among the first she speaks. Say "hi" and wave to her when you enter her room. When you leave, say "bye-bye" and wave again. Have other family members do the same. One day, near her first birthday, you may find your youngster waving back and saying "hi" or "bye-bye."

Vision and Perception

Stacking *Give your baby two or three large, brightly colored blocks; she may try to stack or arrange them. She will begin to compare the blocks and will notice differences in their sizes and colors. If she does not stack them at first, make a three-block tower of your own to show her how. Many children will not stack objects at this age. So if your baby does not seem to understand, you should wait a month or so before encouraging the activity again. Let the youngster simply enjoy handling and moving the blocks in the meanwhile.*

Unwrap it *One at a time, wrap up several toys of various sizes in tissue paper and let your baby unwrap them. Sometimes use a single layer of paper and sometimes several layers. Let her feel the texture of the paper and see how it unfolds. Do not use tape or ribbon.*

Muffin pan puzzle *Most babies love to fit objects inside other objects, an exercise that incidentally helps their eye-hand coordination. You can make a*

good fitting-puzzle using a muffin tin and several tennis balls. Let your baby place the balls in the muffin compartments.

Tub toys *Another pastime that helps develop a baby's eye-hand coordination is playing with objects in the bathtub. Let her drop toys or balls that will float into a floating plastic container. For variation, add other objects such as a sponge or something heavy that sinks. Let her pour water in and out of a cup.*

Emotional and Social

Introducing . . *To help the baby feel comfortable meeting new people, you can make a game out of introductions. When somebody new enters the room, hold the child so she will feel secure. Shake hands with the visitor, then ask the visitor to hand your baby one of her toys. Later you can try to induce the baby to hand something to the visitor. You should let the child decide for herself when she is ready for others to touch her.*

Roll-the-ball *This game develops a sense of teamwork and taking turns as well as muscular coordination. Sit with your legs outstretched, feet touch-*

ing the baby's feet, and roll a ball along the floor to her. Say, "Roll it back to me!" Once your child learns how this game works, try adding a gentle bounce.

Hugging *Now that your baby is becoming aware of expressing herself emotionally, encourage her to show affection toward her dolls and stuffed animals. Pick up a favorite animal and hug it, kiss it or pat it. Then let your baby do the same. Make sure that you hug your child, too, as part of the game.*

Family album *By this age, your child can handle her own family photo scrapbook, instead of making do with your showing her the pictures on the wall. Of course, the pictures must be extra, expendable prints. Place one large photo on each page. If she does not seem to recognize the person in the photo right away when she turns to a page, tell her who it is.*

For the Toy Box

Plastic or metal bowls and cups that stack within one another. A set of wooden blocks in different sizes and colors. Extra-large unwrapped crayons and big sheets of paper for scribbling. Simple jack-in-the-box toys. Surprise activity box with buttons to push, knobs to pull, hinged doors to open.

Bibliography

BOOKS

Avery, Gordon B., M.D., ed., *Neonatology: Pathophysiology and Management of the Newborn.* Philadelphia: J. B. Lippincott, 1981.

Bernath, Maja, *Parents Book for Your Baby's First Year.* New York: Ballantine, 1983.

Bollinger, Taree, and Patricia Cramer, *The Baby Gear Guide.* Reading, Mass.: Addison-Wesley, 1985.

Bower, T.G.R., *Development in Infancy.* San Francisco: W. H. Freeman and Company, 1982.

Brazelton, T. Berry, M.D.:
On Becoming a Family. New York: Dell, 1981.
Infants and Mothers. New York: Dell, 1983.
To Listen to a Child. Reading, Mass.: Addison-Wesley, 1984.

Brewster, Patricia Dorothy, *You Can Breastfeed Your Baby.* Emmaus, Pa.: Rodale Press, 1979.

Brody, Jane, *Jane Brody's Nutrition Book.* New York: Bantam Books, 1981.

Burck, Frances Wells, *Baby Sense.* New York: St. Martin's, 1979.

Burtt, Kent Garland, and Karen Kalkstein, *Smart Toys: For Babies from Birth to Two.* New York: Harper & Row, 1981.

Caplan, Frank, ed., *The First Twelve Months of Life.* New York: Bantam Books, 1973.

Castle, Sue, *Nutrition for Your Child's Most Important Years: Birth to Age Three.* New York: Simon & Schuster, 1984.

Chase, Richard A., M.D., John J. Fisher III and Richard R. Rubin, eds., *Your Baby: The First Wondrous Year.* New York: Macmillan, 1984.

Chess, Stella, M.D., Alexander Thomas, M.D., and Herbert G. Birch, M.D., *Your Child Is a Person.* New York: Viking, 1965.

Church, Joseph, *Understanding Your Child from Birth to Three.* New York: Pocket Books, 1973.

The Commonsense Guide to Birth and Babies, by the Editors of Time-Life Books. New York: Holt, Rinehart and Winston, 1982.

The Complete Baby Book, by the Editors of Consumer Guide. New York: Simon and Schuster, 1979.

Dazé, Anne Marie, R.N., B.S.N., and John W. Scanlon, M.D., *Neonatal Nursing: A Practical Guide.* Baltimore: University Park Press, 1985.

DeLorenzo, Lorisa, and Robert John DeLorenzo, M.D., *Total Child Care: From Birth to Age Five.* Garden City, N.Y.: Doubleday, 1982.

Dunn, Judy, *Distress and Comfort.* Cambridge: Harvard University Press, 1977.

Eagan, Andrea Boroff, *The Newborn Mother: Stages of Her Growth.* Boston: Little, Brown, 1985.

Eden, Alvin N., M.D., *Positive Parenting.* New York: New American Library, 1980.

Eheart, Brenda Krause, and Susan Karol Martel, *The Fourth Trimester: On Becoming a Mother.* New York: Ballantine, 1983.

Eiger, Marvin S., M.D., and Sally Wendkos Olds, *The Complete Book of Breastfeeding.* New York: Bantam Books, 1972.

Fomon, Samuel J., M.D., *Infant Nutrition.* Philadelphia: W. B. Saunders Company, 1974.

Forbes, Gilbert B., M.D., and Calvin W. Woodruff, M.D., eds., *Pediatric Nutrition Handbook.* Elk Grove Village, Ill.: American Academy of Pediatrics, 1985.

Fraiberg, Selma H., *The Magic Years.* New York: Charles Scribner's Sons, 1959.

Gansberg, Judith M., and Arthur P. Mostel, M.D., *The Second Nine Months.* New York: Pocket Books, 1984.

Gerber Library, *500 Questions New Parents Ask.* New York: Dell, 1982.

Goodman, Susan, *You & Your Child.* New York: Exeter Books, 1984.

Gordon, Ira J.:
Baby to Parent, Parent to Baby. New York: St. Martin's, 1977.
Baby Learning Through Baby Play. New York: St. Martin's, 1970.

Grasselli, Rose N., and Priscilla A. Hegner, *Playful Parenting.* New York: Perigee Books, 1981.

Hagstrom, Julie, and Joan Morrill, *Games Babies Play & More Games Babies Play.* New York: Pocket Books, 1981.

Heslin, Jo-Ann, Annette B. Natow and Barbara C. Raven, *No-Nonsense Nutrition for Your Baby's First Year.* Boston: CBI Publishing Company, 1978.

Hillman, Sheilah, *The Baby Checkup Book.* New York: Bantam Books, 1982.

Jones, Sandy:
Crying Baby, Sleepless Nights. New York: Warner Books, 1983.
Good Things for Babies. Boston: Houghton Mifflin, 1980.

Karnes, Merle B., *You and Your Small Wonder.* Circle Pines, Minn.: American Guidance Service, 1982

Kelly, Paula, M.D., ed., *First-Year Baby Care.* Deephaven, Minn.: Meadowbrook Press, 1983.

Klaus, Marshall H., M.D., and John H. Kennell, M.D., *Parent-Infant Bonding.* St. Louis: C. V. Mosby, 1982.

Klaus, Marshall H., M.D., and Phyllis H. Klaus, *The Amazing Newborn.* Reading, Mass.: Addison-Wesley, 1985.

Lansky, Vicki:
Welcoming Your Second Baby. New York: Bantam Books, 1984.
Getting Your Baby to Sleep and Back to Sleep. New York: Bantam Books, 1985.

Lauwers, Judith, and Candace Woessner, *Counseling the Nursing Mother.* Wayne, N.J.: Avery Publishing Group, 1983.

Leach, Penelope:
Your Baby & Child. New York: Knopf, 1983.
Babyhood. New York: Knopf, 1983.

La Leche League International, *The Womanly Art of Breastfeeding.* Franklin Park, Ill.: 1981.

Liman, Ellen, *Babyspace.* New York: Perigee Books, 1983.

McCall, Robert B., *Infants.* Cambridge: Harvard University Press, 1979.

Munger, Evelyn Moats, and Susan Jane Bowdon, *Beyond Peek-A-Boo and Pat-A-Cake.* Piscataway, N.J.: New Century Publishers, 1980.

Mussen, Paul H., ed., *Handbook of Child Psychology.* New York: John Wiley & Sons, 1983.

Painter, Genevieve, *Teach Your Baby.* New York: Simon & Schuster, 1982.

Pantell, Robert H., M.D., James F. Fries, M.D., and Donald M. Vickery, M.D., *Taking Care of Your Child.* Reading, Mass.: Addison-Wesley, 1984.

Papalia, Diane E., and Sally Wendkos Olds, *A Child's World.* New York: McGraw-Hill, 1983.

Pipes, Peggy L., *Nutrition in Infancy and Childhood.* St. Louis: Times Mirror-Mosby, 1985.

Pringle, Sheila M., R.N., and Brenda E. Ramsey, R.N., M.S.N., *Promoting the Health of Children.* St. Louis: C. V. Mosby, 1982.

Pryor, Karen, *Nursing Your Baby.* New York: Pocket Books, 1973.

Pulaski, Mary Ann Spencer, *Your Baby's Mind and How It Grows.* New York: Harper & Row, 1981.

Queenan, John T., M.D., *A New Life.* New York: Van Nostrand Reinhold, 1979.

Reeder, Sharon J., R.N., Luigi Mastroianni, Jr., M.D., and Leonide L. Martin, R.N., *Maternity Nursing.* Philadelphia: J. B. Lippincott, 1983.

Reit, Seymour V., *Sibling Rivalry.* New York: Ballantine, 1985.

Riordan, Jan, R.N., *A Practical Guide to Breastfeeding.* St. Louis: C. V. Mosby, 1983.

Segal, Marilyn, M.D., *Your Child at Play: Birth to One Year.* New York: Newmarket Press, 1985.

Sills, Barbara, and Jeanne Henry, *The Mother to Mother Baby Care Book.* New York: Avon, 1980.

Sparling, Joseph, and Isabelle Lewis, *Learningames for the First Three Years.* New York: Berkley Books, 1979.

Spock, Benjamin, M.D., and Michael B. Rothenberg, M.D., *Baby and Child Care.* New York: Pocket Books, 1985.

Stern, Daniel, *The First Relationship.* Cambridge: Harvard University Press, 1977.

Stern, Loraine, M.D., and Kathleen MacKay, *Off to a Great Start!* New York: W. W. Norton, 1986.

Stoppard, Miriam, M.D., *Day by Day Baby Care.* New York: Willard Books, 1983.

Tronick, Edward, and Lauren Adamson, *Babies as People.* New York: Collier Books, 1980.

White, Burton L., *The First Three Years of Life.* Englewood Cliffs, N.J.: Prentice-Hall, 1975.

Weissbluth, Marc, M.D., *Crybabies: Coping with Colic.* New York: Berkley Books, 1984.

Ziegel, Erna E., R.N., and Mecca S. Cranley, R.N., *Obstetric Nursing.* New York: Macmillan, 1984.

PERIODICALS

Eden, Alvin N., M.D., "Why Do Babies Cry?" *American Baby,* January 1986.

"The First Year of Life." *American Baby,* Mid-May 1980.

Friedrich, Otto, "What Do Babies Know?" *Time,* August 15, 1983.

Gaylin, Jody, "For Crying Out Loud." *Parents,* April 1985.

Hillard, Paula Adams, M.D., "Circumcision." *Parents,* April 1984.

Labson, Lucy H.:
"The Newborn: Quick Postdelivery Check." *Patient Care,* April 30, 1983.
"Newborn Exam: Evaluation in the Nursery." *Patient Care,* May 30, 1983.
"Newborn Exam: Neurologic Evaluation." Patient Care, May 30, 1983.

Lagercrantz, Hugo, and Theodore A. Slotkin, "The 'Stress' of Being Born." *Scientific American,* April 1986.

Levy, Harvey L., and Marvin L. Mitchell, "The Current Status of Newborn Screening."

Hospital Practice, July 1982.

Merlin, Dale, R.N., "Diapering Alternatives." *Baby Talk,* April 1985.

McCall, Robert B.:
"The Dawn of Love." *Parents,* June 1985.
"False Expectations." *Parents,* September 1983.

Pines, Maya, "Baby, You're Incredible." *Psychology Today,* February 1982.

Pomeranz, Virginia E., M.D., and Dodi Schultz:
"You're Going to Spoil That Child!" *Parents,* January 1986.
"Tests for the Newborn Baby." *Parents,* November 1985.

Reid, Joan, "A Look at the Newborn." *American Baby,* May 1986.

Sears, William, M.D.:
"How to Manage the Fussy Baby." *American Baby,* December 1983.
"Understanding Temperament and Sleep." *Baby Talk,* February 1986.

Simon, Nissa, "Skin Problems and Birthmarks." *Parents,* May 1985.

Younger, Janet B., R.N., M.S.N., "The Management of Night Waking in Older Infants." *Pediatric*

Nursing, May/June 1982.

"Your Baby's Growth and Development." *Baby Talk,* March-September 1985.

OTHER PUBLICATIONS

"From A to Z. . .A Policy Reference Guide to AAP Council, Committee, and Executive Board Statements." Elk Grove Village, Ill.: American Academy of Pediatrics, 1984.

Glover, Elayne M., Jodi K. Preminger and Anne R. Sanford, "E-Lap: The Early Learning Accomplishment Profile for Developmentally Young Children — Birth to 36 Months." Winston-Salem, N.C.: Kaplan Press, 1978.

"Growing Child." Lafayette, Ind.: Dunn & Hargitt, April 1985.

Lipsitt, Lewis P., "Playtime with Baby: Baby's First Playground." Pawtucket, R.I.: Playskool, 1986.

"Newborns: Care of the Uncircumcised Penis." Elk Grove Village, Ill.: American Academy of Pediatrics, 1986.

"The Safe Nursery." Washington, D.C.: U.S. Consumer Product Safety Commission, 1985.

Acknowledgments and Picture Credits

The index for this book was prepared by Louise Hedberg. The editors also thank: William John Cochran, M.D., Baylor College of Medicine, Houston; Theresa DeLaFleur, R.N., M.S.N., Alexandria, Va.; Cutberto Garza, M.D., Baylor College of Medicine, Houston; Jane Gwiazda, Massachusetts Institute of Technology, Boston; Libby Hamilton, Alexandria Hospital Library, Alexandria, Va.; Judy Hopkinson, Baylor College of Medicine, Houston; Kathleen Moffitt, R.N., Alexandria Hospital, Alexandria, Va.; Jeff L. Molter, American Academy of Pediatrics, Elk Grove Village, Ill.; Leith Mullaly, R.N., M.S.N., Alexandria Hospital, Alexandria, Va.; Emily Schrag, National Center for Clinical Infant Programs, Washington.

The sources for the photographs in this book are listed below, followed by the sources for the illustrations. Credits from left to right are separated by semicolons, from top to bottom by dashes.

Photographs. Cover, 7-49: Susie Fitzhugh. 51: Neil Kagan. 52: Barbara Campbell. 55: Beecie Kupersmith. 59: Suzanne Szasz. 63: Susie Fitzhugh. 67: Beecie Kupersmith. 71, 77: Susie Fitzhugh. 79: Beecie Kupersmith. 83, 85: Susie Fitzhugh. 94: Beecie Kupersmith. 99: Suzanne Szasz. 103-132: Neil Kagan.

Illustrations. 24: Kathe Scherr from photo by Fran Moshos. 25-29: Kathe Scherr from photos by Neil Kagan. 30: Kathe Scherr from photos by Neil Kagan — Nancy C. Scott. 35: Marguerite E. Bell. 36: Marguerite E. Bell from photos by Neil Kagan. 37: Marguerite E. Bell from photos by Fran Moshos; Neil Kagan(2) — Beecie Kupersmith. 39: Marguerite E. Bell. 41: Marguerite E. Bell from photos by Neil Kagan — Marguerite E. Bell. 43: Marguerite E. Bell from photo by Beecie Kupersmith. 44: Marguerite E. Bell from photos by Fran Moshos. 45: Marguerite E. Bell from photos by Susie Fitzhugh(2); Beecie Kupersmith. 46: Marguerite E. Bell. 47: Marguerite E. Bell from photos by Neil Kagan; Beecie Kupersmith — Neil Kagan(2). 48: Marguerite E. Bell from photos by Fran Moshos. 50: Marguerite E. Bell from photos by Neil Kagan. 53: Marguerite E. Bell from photo by Beecie Kupersmith. 54: Marguerite E. Bell from photo by Neil Kagan. 64: Jane Hurd from photo by Susie Fitzhugh. 65: Donald Gates, adapted from "Breast Feeding Your Baby." American College of Obstetricians and Gynecologists Patient Education Pamphlet p-029, Washington: ACOG, 1983. 66: Donald Gates from photos by Beecie Kupersmith. 67: Donald Gates from photos by Beecie Kupersmith — Susie Fitzhugh. 68, 69: Donald Gates from photos by Beecie Kupersmith. 72: Donald Gates. 73, 74: Donald Gates from photos by Neil Kagan. 75: Donald Gates from photos by Beecie Kupersmith — Beecie Kupersmith; Neil Kagan. 78: Donald Gates. 80, 82: Donald Gates from photos by Beecie Kupersmith. 91-97: Kathe Scherr from photos by Beecie Kupersmith. 105-113: Kathe Scherr from photos by Neil Kagan. 115: Kathe Scherr from photos by Neil Kagan; Margaret Palmquist — Neil Kagan. 116-137: Kathe Scherr from photos by Neil Kagan.

Index

Time-Life Books Inc. offers a wide range of fine recordings, including a *Big Bands* series. For subscription information, call 1-800-621-7026, or write TIME-LIFE MUSIC,
Time & Life Building, Chicago, Illinois 60611.